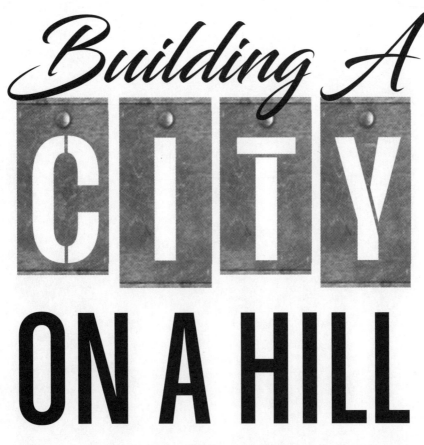

Building A CITY ON A HILL

African American Communities of Purpose

Student Workbook

Written and Edited by Kwasi I. Kena, D.Min.

UMI (Urban Ministries, Inc.)
P. O. Box 436987
Chicago, Illinois 60643-6987
1-800-860-8642
www.urbanministries.com

First Edition

First Printing

Scripture quotations marked KJV, or unmarked, are from King James Version.

Scripture quotations marked NIV are taken from the HOLY BIBLE, NEW INTERNATIONAL VERSION®, copyright © 1973, 1978, 1984, 2011. Used by permission of Zondervan. All rights reserved.

Scripture quotations marked NASB are taken from the NEW AMERICAN STANDARD BIBLE®, COPYRIGHT © 1960, 1962, 1963, 1971, 1972, 1973, 1975, 1977, 1995 by The Lockman Foundation. Used by permission.

Library of Congress Cataloguing in Publications Data

Building A City On A Hill: African American Communities of Purpose Student Workbook
ISBN-13: 978-1-68353-129-6

Printed in the United States of America.

Dedication

To Irene "Dr. Auntie" Goggans, honored for her work as a community historian who tirelessly archived Milwaukee's Black history to ensure *our story* was told and preserved.

Table of Contents

Introduction

Building is a creative endeavor. If asked to construct a house, a business, or a community from scratch, few of us could complete the task without some outside assistance. The creation accounts in Genesis chapters 1 and 2 introduce us to God, the Creator. God created the heavens and earth, *ex nihilo* (out of nothing). The work was ecologically friendly—nothing God created harmed another part of creation. The work was thoughtful—every part of creation had a complementary function. The work was satisfying—God said "It is good." Then God created humankind as co-creators to steward the earth's resources and care for what God created.

As Christians, we must remember that God's original call to be co-laborers remains in effect. The Lord expects us to participate in building the kingdom of God. We cannot do it by ourselves. We need help from the Master Planner. With God's help, we can discern the tasks to perform, identify the people and resources needed, and imagine what the godly outcomes of work should be.

The lessons contained in this *Building A City On A Hill Student Workbook* will invite you to discover essential components needed to build strong families, churches, and communities. Jesus, Abraham, Moses, Jethro, Rahab, and Joshua will be our guides. Each of these biblical characters will teach us an important lesson about developing personal character, expressing concern for others, and serving God's purposes.

During His earthly ministry, Jesus constantly referred to the kingdom of God through parables and teachings. Building the kingdom was the central message of Jesus' ministry. Over 2,000 years later, we also should be focusing on what it means to build God's kingdom through worshipful work in our homes, on our jobs, at our churches, and in our communities.

The book *Building A City On A Hill* provides rich history and backstory of ten Black towns built by people of African descent. Each of those stories contains insights about community building. The big-picture concepts in *Building A City On A Hill,* coupled with the biblical insights explored in this *Student Workbook,* will prompt you to imagine how to build God's kingdom in our twenty-first century context.

With Jesus Christ as our Master Builder, let us begin our journey toward building strong families, strong churches, and strong communities.

HOW TO USE THIS STUDENT WORKBOOK

Use the *Building A City On A Hill Student Workbook* in conjunction with the Black history book, *Building A City On A Hill*. This *Student Workbook* provides content designed to deepen your understanding of the principles around building the kingdom of God.

This Workbook offers the following study tools:

- **MEMORY VERSE:** To develop internalization and knowledge of God's Word.

- **INTRODUCTION:** To introduce a major feature of the lesson using biblical, historical, or contemporary illustrations.

- **BLACK HISTORY SPOTLIGHT:** To highlight a Black town and draw principles from the story that are relevant today.

- **LESSON FOCUS:** To highlight the primary learning emphasis of the lesson.

- **BIBLE BACKGROUND:** To provide insights about the biblical terms, concepts, or characters mentioned in the background Scripture reading.

- **SCRIPTURE EXPLORATION:** To reflect on how principles from the passage influence your thoughts, beliefs, and behaviors.

- **CONTEMPORARY COMMUNITY DEVELOPMENT:** To connect the lesson to a contemporary ministry that demonstrates practical application of some aspect of the lesson.

- **DISCUSSION:** To help you personally engage with lessons from the Scripture passage and apply God's Word practically to your daily life, the following categories guide you in further reflection. The "What" section helps pinpoint the fundamental teachings from the lesson. The "So What" section encourages deeper reflection about selected topics from the lesson.

- **APPLICATION OF SCRIPTURE:** To promote further thinking about ways to apply the lesson objectives to your personal life and to the life of the congregation.

- **MEDITATION:** To provide a meditative thought to close each session and offer participants a written meditation to reference during their personal devotions.

- **PRAYER:** To provide a prayerful thought to close each session and offer participants a written prayer to reference during their personal devotions.

We encourage you to respond to each question listed in the "Discussion" and "Application of Scripture" sections to enhance your learning experience. For your review, an answer key for the Discussion Questions for each chapter is provided in the back of the book.

CHAPTER 1

Build On Jesus

Scripture Lesson: Matthew 7:24-27
Background Scriptures: Matthew 7:15-27

MEMORY VERSE

Therefore everyone who hears these words of mine and puts them into practice is like a wise man who built his house on the rock. (Matthew 7:24, NIV)

QUESTION

1. Can you recall a time when you were part of a building project (home, church, business)? What major decisions did you and others make before deciding to begin the project?

2. What conditions had to be met before beginning construction?

INTRODUCTION

Jesus expects Christians to count the cost of discipleship. Discipleship requires consideration of personal and community responsibilities. The parable in today's lesson reveals this to us. Jesus tells us to build our lives on a solid foundation. Some read Scripture solely to improve their individual lives. Discipleship involves more than personal faith development, however. We all belong to communities that need God's redemptive power. Jesus commissions us to be the "salt of the earth" and the "light of the world." Our witness to Christ involves both a personal and communal vision. How then shall we serve the Lord?

One way to serve God is through community building. The Bible contains practical answers for community and government leaders. Just as God molded Israel into a nation, a chosen special people, God expects contemporary Christians to participate in advancing the kingdom of God on earth—now. People of African descent have long participated in our own community-building endeavors by founding towns before and after emancipation.

In this series, we will explore Scripture to discover God's practical guidance for personal and communal discipleship and we will examine ten towns founded by African Americans that illustrate vital steps to take for societal development.

BLACK HISTORY SPOTLIGHT: Mound Bayou

The story of Mound Bayou, one of the first incorporated Black towns in the United States, is a prime example of Black families and communities working together to establish a legacy for generations to come. Dreams of establishing a colony in Mississippi were helped by industrialization. During Reconstruction, southern states began to industrialize and they started to strengthen their transportation networks, a transition that opened new territories for exploration. Railroad companies wanted to make inroads into the uncultivated lands of the Mississippi Delta. These railroads needed laborers in the areas of the uncultivated land. Isaiah Montgomery, the founding pioneer of Mound Bayou, seized this opportunity. Together with his cousin Benjamin Green, he purchased more than 800 acres of land on the grounds where the railroad was to expand.

To survive the American frontier, Mound Bayou's residents worked diligently to establish a strong foundation. It was located in the northwestern part of Mississippi, a region so undeveloped it had been referred to as a "dense jungle." The new residents cleared forest and constructed roads. The first settlers to the area were not ordinary farmers or businessmen; they were men and women committed to their dreams. Isaiah Montgomery recruited families from across the country, promising them solitude and an opportunity to have a life outside White control. Eventually, African Americans from all parts of Mississippi and other states came to Mound Bayou.

Removed from the threat of violence, and protected by the town founders' amicable relationships with prominent Southern White men, Mound Bayou thrived as a place where Black people purchased land and set up homesteads.

Booker T. Washington estimated that by 1910, the area included more than 30,000 acres, "all owned by Negroes, most of them small farmers who till 40- and 80-acre tracts." By 1910, the town population had increased to about 500 residents. It is estimated that the larger, surrounding area included approximately 800 families and 4000 people.

Within twenty years, the value of Mound Bayou's land had increased substantially and residents had established a sustainable community. Residents in the town and countryside also found all their basic necessities within the town. By 1910, more than 50 stores and shops existed in the town (*New York Times*, June 12, 1910), including several grocery and carpentry stores, as well as insurance and real estate agencies. The high point of economic development in Mound Bayou occurred in January, 1904, when the town leaders organized and opened Bank of Mound Bayou. The bank provided loans to local residents to help them establish businesses. The bank also provided loans for people to repair their houses.

Mound Bayou reveals the myriad of ways God provides even in the midst of difficult situations. The experiences of the pioneers at Mound Bayou point us to the reality of renewal. Communities rise from the dust as they rededicate themselves. Benjamin Montgomery may have lost the Davis plantation, but his community acquired something even better.

.

SCRIPTURE REFERENCES

(Matthew 7:24-27, NIV)

24 "Therefore everyone who hears these words of mine and puts them into practice is like a wise man who built his house on the rock. 25 The rain came down, the streams rose, and the winds blew and beat against that house; yet it did not fall, because it had its foundation on the rock. 26 But everyone who hears these words of mine and does not put them into practice is like a foolish man who built his house on sand. 27 The rain came down, the streams rose, and the winds blew and beat against that house, and it fell with a great crash."

LESSON FOCUS

Salvation is free, but Christian discipleship is costly. Counting the cost is a sober exercise embraced by disciplined people. Olympic athletes must commit to rigorous training. Military personnel must be willing to give their lives in service. Musicians must commit to long hours of practice. What does Jesus expect of His followers? What does the Lord require of us individually and collectively? How should communities benefit from our Christian witness and service? Keep these questions in mind as we explore the parable from Matthew 7.

BIBLE BACKGROUND

In today's lesson, Jesus focuses attention on how to build what lasts. Constructing a house requires forethought about the associated costs. Likewise, we must count the costs involved with following Christ.

Today's passage, Matthew 7:24-27, is located at the end of the Sermon on the Mount. The sermon consists of three parts. First, we find the Beatitudes (blessings). Part one concludes with Christ commissioning His followers to be "salt of the earth" and "light of the world" (Matthew 5:13-16). Part two highlights the way to eternal life. (Matthew 5:17-7:12) Here we see Jesus as teacher, affirming the authority of the Hebrew Scriptures, while affirming His authority as interpreter of Scripture. We also see the distinction of Jesus' righteousness from that of the Pharisees.

In part three, Jesus highlights the cost of discipleship. Life has narrow and wide gates, and smooth and rough roads (Matthew 7:13-14). He warns His followers of false prophets, instructing them to examine their fruit and judge their validity (Matthew 7:16-20). His closing warning emphasizes the seriousness of discipleship. Jesus says, "Not everyone who says to me, 'Lord, Lord,' will enter the kingdom of heaven, but only the one who does the will of my Father who is in heaven" (Matthew 7:21). Professions of faith without appropriate changes of lifestyle prove empty.[1] The parable of the wise and foolish builders follows Jesus' warning.

SCRIPTURE EXPLORATION

Matthew 7:24-27 is the second part of a dialog Jesus had with people who claimed to follow Him, but refused to follow His teachings. The parable about the wise and

---

[1] Dockery, D. S., Butler, T. C., Church, C. L., Scott, L. L., Ellis Smith, M. A., White, J. E., & Holman Bible Publishers (Nashville, T. . (1992). *Holman Bible Handbook* (p. 548). Nashville, TN: Holman Bible Publishers.

foolish builders begins after this warning in verse 21, "Not everyone who says to me, 'Lord, Lord,' will enter the kingdom of heaven, but only the one who does the will of my Father who is in heaven."

In the parable that follows, constructing a house is a metaphor for a person deciding to follow Jesus Christ. With what forethought and quality of materials will the builder construct the house? What preparations does this construction require? Is the builder prepared to pay the cost of construction?

Today, building projects in developing countries are no less perilous than they were in biblical times. Take, for example, some families in parts of Ghana who have a monthly income of less than $70. What is the cost for them to build a house? Each question is crucial. How much is a bag of concrete? How many concrete blocks will that bag produce? How much sand could be added before compromising the strength of the concrete? If the builder cut corners on the concrete-to-sand mixture, the building might collapse. Considering the cost of construction can be a life-and-death decision for the builder and those who may occupy the structure.

Jesus' audience knew about the serious choices involved with building a house. Some chose to build houses along the wadis in Israel. A wadi was a dry riverbed— at least for most of the year. When rains came, the ground could not absorb the water quickly. This led to flash floods that could wash away the mud homes. The individual choice of construction location affected the community, too. Think of builders who irresponsibly construct homes in known flood plains. The individual decisions we make can create far-reaching detriment to the larger community. Only foolish people would build mud homes in a flood zone. In contrast, wise builders construct homes on rocks to preserve them from sudden floods.

CONTEMPORARY COMMUNITY BUILDING: Pastor Floyd Flake and Greater Allen Cathedral

The Greater Allen A.M.E. Cathedral of New York is one of the largest churches in the United States with 23,000 members. But church membership is only the tip of the iceberg when it comes to the impact that Pastor Floyd Flake and his congregation have had on the borough of Queens in New York city. This church is a pioneer when it comes to having a vision for the community. This church is an institutional landmark and owns subsidiary corporations with an operating budget of $34 million. Its services and commercial enterprises include commercial and residential developments. The corporations, church administrative offices, and ministries comprise one of Queens' largest private sector employers.[2]

DISCUSSION

"WHAT" - THE BASICS

1. Read Matthew 7:21-23. What explicit behavior does Jesus warn against?

---

[2] http://allencathedral.org/allen-ame-floyd-flake/

2. How do you believe this warning relates to the parable of the wise and foolish builders?

3. What point is Jesus making in this parable?

"SO WHAT" - DIGGING DEEPER

1. Taken together, what are the warning and the parable in Matthew 7 saying to you about being a disciple of Jesus Christ?

2. What has following Christ cost you?

3. After examining today's passage, what do you believe God is asking you to do, be, or change?

APPLICATION OF SCRIPTURE

"NOW WHAT?" – ACTION STEPS

Personal

Create a list of the costs of Christian discipleship. Take each item and turn it into a profession. For example, if you listed giving up selfish desires, you could write, "Today, I surrender my desires to you, Lord." Include some declaration of self-government in your list. For example, "I renew my commitment to serve Christ by serving others today." Use your list as a faith declaration throughout the week. Be prepared to share at the next session.

Congregational

Invite the pastor, church leaders, and community-minded individuals to read the descriptions of the eight principles on the Christian Community Development

Association (CCDA) website (See the URL at the end of this chapter under Recommended Resources).

- Relocation

- Reconciliation

- Redistribution

- Leadership Development

- Empowerment

- Wholistic Approach

- Church-Based

- Listening to the Community

Discuss these eight principles and talk about ways to incorporate them into your congregation's ministry practices. Use the following question to launch your brainstorming session.

What could our congregation do to make a difference in the lives of people in our community?

Consider sending several persons from your congregation to one of CCDA's yearly conferences. To learn the backstory on CCDA's philosophy and its founder, John Perkins, read, as a group, *With Justice for All: A Strategy for Community Development* by John Perkins. Afterward, discuss ways to implement his 3 R's for community development: Relocation, Reconciliation, and Redistribution.

MEDITATION

A house on rock, or a house on sand? Life is a series of decisions, and our everyday choices determine our long-term outcomes. Some diligently save over decades for retirement, while others hope to win the lottery before retirement season comes. Some monitor their nutrition and physical activity, while others consume in excess. Some are wise and gracious with their words, while others post foolishness on social media. Some conscientiously love God and neighbor, while others care only for themselves. Each decision brings consequences; either to one's benefit or detriment. Lord, help us to count the cost of each decision we make.

PRAYER

Dear Lord, You paid a costly price for us on Calvary's cross and offer salvation freely. We say "yes" to your offer, and understand no empty claim to Christ will last. You expect Your disciples to follow in Your footsteps. Have we done that? After our "Yes, Lord," have we chosen to live as Christian disciples daily? Teach us Lord. Teach our hands to give, our mouths to bless, and our hearts to love. Through Jesus Christ we pray. Amen.

BIBLIOGRAPHY

Bonhoeffer, Dietrich. *The Cost of Discipleship*. New York: Touchstone. Translated from the German *Nachfolge* first published 1937 by Chr. Kaiser Verlag München by R. H. Fuller, with some revision by Irmgard Booth. Touchstone edition, 1959.

Boomershine, Tom, A Storytelling Commentary on Luke 14:25-33, Retrieved 8/13/2017, http://gotell.org/wp-content/uploads/Mt07_21-29_commentary.pdf)

Dockery, D. S., Butler, T. C., Church, C. L., Scott, L. L., Ellis Smith, M. A., White, J. E., & Holman Bible Publishers (Nashville, T. . (1992). Holman Bible Handbook (p. 548). Nashville, TN: Holman Bible Publishers.

Lenski, R. C. H. (1961). The Interpretation of St. Luke's Gospel (p. 785). Minneapolis, MN: Augsburg Publishing House.

RECOMMENDED RESOURCES:

Christian Community Development Association Philosophy https://ccda.org/about/philosophy/

Perkins, John. *With Justice for All: A Strategy for Community Development*. Ventura, CA: Regal, 2011 (Revised Updated Edition).

CHAPTER 2
Building A Nation

Scripture Lesson: Genesis 12:1-3
Background Scriptures: Genesis 12: 1-4, 17:1-5

MEMORY VERSE

For he was looking forward to the city with foundations, whose architect and builder is God. (Hebrews 11:10, NIV)

QUESTION

Families and friends teach us values and morals. They also play a major part in how we shape our initial attitudes about God. What attitudes toward God did your family system and friends promote? How did they prepare you to hear from and follow God?

INTRODUCTION

In her book *The Call to the Soul*, Marjorie Zoet Bankson writes about four critical questions people ask during their lives: 1. Who am I? 2. What is my work (i.e. vocation or calling)? 3. What is my gift (for sharing with others)? 4. What is my legacy? In today's passage, we find God speaking to 75-year-old Abram. At that stage of life, the legacy question confronted Abram.

In ancient times, as in many countries today, children were essential to one's legacy. Children continued the family name and were the Social Security system for the elderly. When the Lord appeared to Abram, he and Sarai were childless.

God's promise to make Abram a "great nation" meant they would have children. Children ensured Abram a legacy.

To secure this legacy, Abram had to embark on a faith journey to a land God promises to show him *sometime* in the future. God also promised to bless him, and to make his name great. Little did Abram know that more than 25 years would pass before these blessings would manifest. (See Genesis 17.) In today's lesson, we will explore what it means to be called into a defining experience that forms the foundation for greater achievements in life.

BLACK HISTORY SPOTLIGHT:
Seneca Village in New York City, New York

In the late 1700s and early 1800s, New York City Blacks congregated in traditional Black neighborhoods such as Five Points, Yorkville, or near the ports. The opportunities to purchase land were not easy; many landowners were unwilling to sell to even affluent

Blacks. Since Black men had to own more than $250 in property to vote, prominent Blacks understood that they needed to buy land so that they could vote. Places like Seneca Village provided the opportunity to purchase land, and along with it, the opportunity to exercise a right of citizenship: voting. One of the best opportunities for Blacks to do this happened when speculators purchased large farming tracks near urban centers and subdivided it. By subdividing larger tracts into small ones, speculators wanted to earn money fast. They were willing to make quick money by selling to Blacks who wanted to own property. John and Elizabeth Whitehead purchased farmland in an area between West 82nd and West 85th streets and between Seventh and Eighth avenues. This was land outside the city core, which meant the number of people living there was less. It was also likely cheaper than what a lot might cost in the city. The Black people who purchased lots in Seneca Village looked forward, envisioning what they could accomplish politically and economically for their community and for future generations. They assessed the cost of their dream and went after it.

Unfortunately, Seneca Village was destroyed as part of a larger citywide plan to create Central Park. Nonetheless, the legacy of education and the church left an imprint on the African American community, demonstrating that churches and communities that work together can accomplish much. The repossession of Seneca Village in 1856 was yet another example of how local government has the ability to force people off their land to provide for projects that would provide services for elite White communities. Indeed, many Blacks had moved to Seneca Village after being removed from York Hill, which was destroyed to establish a water system for New York City. Nonetheless, Seneca Village demonstrates that Black people, even under harsh conditions, continued to find ways to strengthen their communities.

SCRIPTURE REFERENCES

(Genesis 12:1-3, NIV)

[1] The Lord had said to Abram, "Go from your country, your people and your father's household to the land I will show you. [2] "I will make you into a great nation, and I will bless you; I will make your name great, and you will be a blessing. [3] I will bless those who bless you, and whoever curses you I will curse; and all peoples on earth will be blessed through you."

LESSON FOCUS

Today's passage reveals God inviting Abram into a journey of faith. The destination is unknown. The impetus for going is trust. The reward is promised blessings. God's invitation requires Abram to leave his home, country, and kinfolk. He must leave all that is familiar to experience the unknown. Faith journeys ask us to do more than we think we are capable of doing, as is the case for this childless, elderly couple, Abram and Sarai. Faith journeys demand belief despite the odds. In today's lesson, we will explore the beginning of what will become a decades-long journey, during which Abram's faith will be tested and matured.

BIBLE BACKGROUND

Genesis chapter 12 marks a shift in the spiritual narrative of the Hebrews. Before this, the Genesis featured God's interactions with individuals like Adam and Eve, Cain and Able, or Noah and his sons. God's interaction with Abram is different. God invites him into a faith journey that will culminate in a covenant that creates a nation. The Abrahamic Covenant establishes the spiritual foundation of Israel—God's covenant people.

With covenant comes responsibility. Faith now takes center stage—"Go from your country, your people, and your father's household to the land I will show you" (Genesis 12:1). Following closely behind faith is hope—"I *will* make you into a great nation, I *will* bless you." (Genesis 12:2b, emphasis added). Hope draws us into the future; faith sustains us in the present.

SCRIPTURE EXPLORATION

Imagine if the Lord told you to leave your hometown and your family and friends to go to another country—details to follow later. That, in essence, is what Abram experienced. God's invitation demanded a faith response from him. Abram must leave his country, his people, *and* his father's household. Consider the challenges involved with leaving your hometown to become a pioneer.

Some of you may have family stories about your kinfolk who courageously participated in the Great Migration of African Americans from 1910 to 1970. Unfair labor practices like sharecropping, tenant farming, and the crop-lien system, motivated more than six million African Americans to migrate from the South to urban centers in the North, Midwest, and West.[1] The journey was difficult. Legalized segregation imposed hardships on these pioneers. They were routinely denied lodging and service at restaurants, and were arbitrarily arrested.

To counter this discrimination, Victor Hugo Green, a mailman from New York City, created *The Negro Motorist Green Book* (later known as *The Green Book*). This annual guidebook, published from 1936-1964, listed establishments across the U.S. (and eventually several international destinations) that welcomed Black people. The establishments included hotels, boarding houses, restaurants, beauty salons, and barbershops. Once these pioneers established themselves, they provided safe havens for the next wave of travelers. Through Green's efforts, many African Americans were blessed to find safe places to lodge and food to eat on their journey from the South.

Abram also faced peril traveling through unknown territories. Before embarking, however, he first had to choose to leave his kinfolk. Why would God tell Abram to leave his home country and kinfolk? We find a plausible answer in the book of Joshua. "This is what the LORD, the God of Israel, says: 'Long ago your ancestors, including Terah the father of Abraham and

---

[1] History.com Staff. Great Migration. 2010. History.com. http://www.history.com/topics/black-history/great-migration. Accessed September 8, 2017.

Nahor, lived beyond the Euphrates River and worshiped other gods" (Joshua 24:2).

Counselors might refer to Abram's separation from his close relations as the "differentiation of self." This separation is necessary as some people become so entangled in their family's feelings and beliefs that they fail to develop their own identity. Differentiated persons can reflect calmly on conflict, note their role in the conflict, and make responsible choices. Abram's family worshiped other gods; that created spiritual conflict between Abram and God. God's invitation to leave gave Abram the opportunity to choose a destiny defined by faith in God. Faithful discipleship requires putting God first— even over family.

In verse 2, the conversation shifts from the present to the future as the Lord utters a series of "I will" statements. There is no mention of when in the future these promises will become reality. Nevertheless, promises like these stir hope for a better future. God promises to make Abram a great nation. Abram's name will be great. All the peoples on earth will be blessed through him. Our faithful actions affect the welfare of others. God created humankind to be interdependent. Our actions affect others.

Through this covenant with Abram, God establishes a people. They will be distinguished from other peoples by their covenant-relationship with God. Abram's willingness to follow God created the opportunity for the foundation of Israel's faith.

CONTEMPORARY COMMUNITY BUILDING: Rev. Cynthia Hale and Ray of Hope Church

Rev. Cynthia Hale is the senior pastor and the founder of Ray of Hope Church in Decatur, Georgia. Rev. Hale is also the secretary for the Hampton Ministers Conference. The church is active in the community and provides medical clinics to different underserved populations. The outreach ministry provides clinics for the homeless and victims of commercial sexual exploitation. The ministry also offers programs for the homeless and advocates for justice reform and reentry assistance for the formerly incarcerated.

DISCUSSION

"WHAT" - THE BASICS

1. What from today's lesson was most challenging to you?

2. The Lord told Abram to leave his country, his people, and his father's household. How challenging would it be for you to do this? Provide specific examples.

3. Think about the attachments that you have established: friends, family, comfort with the familiar, etc. What would it take to convince you to accept God's invitation to leave these close relationships and go to an unfamiliar place?

4. What type of response do you think your family and friends would have if you told them you were leaving your hometown and your country to go where God was leading you?

"SO WHAT" - DIGGING DEEPER

1. What type of spiritual maturity would it take for you to do what Abram did? Describe what would prepare you to trust God in this situation.

2. Abram had to leave his father's household behind to follow God. When family desires conflict with God's principles, how do you handle those situations? Provide examples.

3. The covenant God initiated with Abram would eventually bless nations. In what ways do you believe your allegiance to Jesus Christ can bless others?

4. In today's passage, God said to Abram, "I will bless those who bless you . . . and all peoples on earth will be blessed through you." What about Abram do you believe would cause God to make such a promise?

APPLICATION OF SCRIPTURE

"NOW WHAT?" – ACTION STEPS

Personal

Create an altar in your home. Think of it as a sacred place to refocus your attention on your relationship with Jesus Christ. Place items on the altar that remind you of your Christian faith: a cross, a Bible, etc. List the attachments that you have established: friends, family, job, favorite establishments, etc. Place this list of attachments on your altar. Ask God to help you release the grip of these attachments to prepare you for greater service to the Lord. Monitor your feelings about these attachments in a journal. Write about how willing you believe you are to leave your attachments behind to serve the Lord more completely.

Congregational

Visit the ministries section of the Windsor Village Church website (www.kingdombuilders.com/ministries/). Note the emphasis the church places on community development. Brainstorm with the pastor, leaders, and other members of your church ways your congregation could engage in community development activities.

1. Identify the assets you have inside the church family: facilities, finances, expertise, social networks, etc. How might you harness these assets to create educational programs, social awareness events, or outreach programs?

2. Identify the assets available in your community such as the following: Facilities—like Boys and Girls Clubs, YMCAs, community centers, parks etc.; Human Resources—business owners, professionals, fraternities and sororities, professional organizations.

How might you partner with one or more of these groups to create educational programs, social awareness events, or outreach programs?

For more information about identifying potential assets, conduct an online search using the term "asset mapping." (For further reading, consider *The Power of Asset Mapping* listed in Recommended Resources below.)

MEDITATION

Lord, sometimes I am torn between two loyalties. The family that nurtured and cared for me sometimes expects me to give them the first fruits of my time, energy, and devotion. Your call compels me, their demands consume me. I love them, yet I know I must love You more. Your desire to bless others through me weighs in the balance. When I am stretched between two loyalties, quiet my heart, draw me away to hear, and grant me the courage to act for the sake of the kingdom of God.

PRAYER

Dear Lord, call me and I will answer. Lead me, and I will follow. Send me, and I will go. Show me the faces of those who need Your love. Burn their images into my mind so that I cannot ignore the call to love God and love neighbor. Today I choose to make myself available so You can bless others through me. Amen.

BIBLIOGRAPHY

Bankson, Marjorie Zoet. *The Call to the Soul*. Minneapolis: Augsburg Books, 2005.

Goodavage, Maria. 'Green Book' Helped Keep African Americans Safe on the Road. January 10, 2013. www.pbs.org. http://www.pbs.org/independentlens/blog/green-book-helped-keep-african-americans-safe-on-the-road/ Accessed September 8, 2017.

History.com Staff. Great Migration. 2010. History.com. http://www.history.com/topics/black-history/great-migration. Accessed September 8, 2017.

Nichols, Michael P. and Richard C. Schwartz. *Family Therapy: Concepts and Methods (11th Edition)*. Carmel, Indiana: Pearson, 2016.

Tunnell, Harry. The Negro Motorist Green Book (1936-1964). www.blackpast.org. http://www.blackpast.org/aah/negro-motorist-green-book-1936-1964 Accessed September 8, 2017.

RECOMMENDED RESOURCES:

Goodavage, Maria. 'Green Book' Helped Keep African Americans Safe on the Road. January 10, 2013. www.pbs.org. http://www.pbs.org/independentlens/blog/green-book-helped-keep-african-americans-safe-on-the-road/ Accessed September 8, 2017.

History.com Staff. Great Migration. 2010. History.com. http://www.history.com/topics/black-history/great-migration. Accessed September 8, 2017.

Snow, Luther K. *The Power of Asset Mapping: How Your Congregation Can Act on Its Gifts*. Lanham, Maryland: Rowan & Littlefield, 2004.

Windsor Village Church website http://www.kingdombuilders.com/ministries/

NOTES

CHAPTER 3

Building Strong Families

Scripture Lesson: Genesis 17:5-9
Background Scriptures: Genesis 17:1-22

MEMORY VERSE

Religion that God our Father accepts as pure and faultless is this: to look after orphans and widows in their distress and to keep oneself from being polluted by the world. (James 1:27, NIV)

QUESTION

If someone asked you to describe the characteristics of a strong family, what would you say? Think of specific beliefs, and behaviors that make families strong.

INTRODUCTION

In the previous session, we saw God invite Abram into relationship. Abram responded in faith; he left his homeland and kinfolk. Centuries later, the writer of Hebrews recounts Abram's faithful action. "By faith Abraham, when called to go to a place he would later receive as his inheritance, obeyed and went, even though he did not know where he was going" (Hebrews 11:10). Faith in God became the foundation upon which Abram built his life.

Today's Bible lesson occurs nearly 25 years after God's initial invitation. During that time, he and Sarai remained childless. This tested his faith. He and Sarai took matters into their own hands. At Sarai's bidding, Abram tried to produce an heir through his slave, Hagar, instead of trusting God to give him a son through his wife, Sarai (Genesis 16:1-6). Building strong faith involves learning from one's mistakes. Was Abram ready now? Had he matured enough spiritually? God's covenant-relationship demanded more from him, because the covenant involved both Abram and his descendants.

BLACK HISTORY SPOTLIGHT: Sweet Home, Texas

George W. Smith, head of the Freedmen's Bureau, a government organization that assisted former slaves and others affected by the war, wrote about the majority of White people in Guadalupe County, Texas and the surrounding region. They wanted "to keep the blacks in the same relations to them as when in slavery." Although the period started rough, things did not stay that way. By the 1880s, Blacks in Guadalupe County had established strong communities and settlements. Indeed, Guadalupe County included a number of small settlements, often comprised of less than sixty persons each. As Smith noted, education was not easy for Blacks in Guadalupe County to procure. Nevertheless, by 1880 much progress had been made, particularly in the larger settlements. Two of the larger Black settlements in Guadalupe County were Sweet Home and Jakes Colony. According to historians, Sweet Home was settled by former slaves and the first school was organized in a log cabin. The first mention of a school at Sweet Home came in the 1870s when it was noted that Sweet Home "had four months of school with Ellen Clark as teacher." This was one more month of education compared to the other settlements such as Zion Hill or Randolph that only held school for three months. In 1924, residents of Sweet Home raised enough money to receive additional funding from the Rosenwald Foundation to establish a Rosenwald Trade School. In addition to this school, there were eventually five other Rosenwald Schools in Guadalupe County, demonstrating the residents' dedication to pursuing education.[1]

Although Guadalupe County's Black community has fewer members today than it did in the early twentieth century, the Black residents of the county have tremendous pride in the churches and schools their ancestors created.

---

[1] Josephine S. Etlinger, *Sweetest You Can Find: Life in Eastern Guadalupe County, Texas, 1851–1951* (San Antonio: Watercress, 1987), 182; For a list of all Rosenwald Schools throughout the country please consult the Rosenwald searchable database at Fisk University, http://rosenwald.fisk.edu.

SCRIPTURE REFERENCES

(Genesis 17:5-9, NIV)

5 No longer will you be called Abram; your name will be Abraham, for I have made you a father of many nations. 6 I will make you very fruitful; I will make nations of you, and kings will come from you. 7 I will establish my covenant as an everlasting covenant between me and you and your descendants after you for the generations to come, to be your God and the God of your descendants after you. 8 The whole land of Canaan, where you now reside as a foreigner, I will give as an everlasting possession to you and your descendants after you; and I will be their God." 9 Then God said to Abraham, "As for you, you must keep my covenant, you and your descendants after you for the generations to come."

LESSON FOCUS

We began this session by asking you to describe the characteristics of a strong family. Counselors agree that strong families communicate well, encourage each other, and spend quality time together. They have clearly defined roles and express appreciation. Commitment is an essential characteristic that binds families together. Members of strong families commit to each other and to their religious affiliations. The latter commitment involves more than church membership and regular worship attendance. Strong families express their religious commitment through "concern for others, involvement in worthy causes, or adherence to a moral code."[2]

God's covenant demanded this type of commitment from Abraham and his descendants. God also expects Christian churches and para-church organizations to express this commitment through their compassion ministries. Today's lesson focuses on the ways covenant relationship with God establishes our identity and purpose.

BIBLE BACKGROUND

Scripture frequently mentions the term "covenant." The closest English equivalent to it is "promise." Bible writers used "covenant" as the primary metaphor to describe the relation between God and the people of Israel. Covenant establishes the rule (or kingdom) of God. Thus, covenant helps us understand the biblical ideal of religious community.[3]

A covenant relationship is not merely a mutual acquaintance but a commitment to responsibility and action.[4] It took time for Abram to assume the responsibilities required by God's covenant. Genesis 15:1-6 marked a pivotal change in Abram's relationship with God. When God again told Abram that his reward would be great, Abram reminded God that he and Sarai were still childless. God then rehearsed the promise; Abram's descendants would be as numerous as the stars. Finally, Abram believed God would give him and Sarai a son and start a family of their own. Faith was taking root.

SCRIPTURE EXPLORATION

Today's passage introduces us to the Abrahamic Covenant. This covenant between God and Abraham marked a change in their relationship. God changed Abram's name from Abram, "exalted father," to Abraham, "father of many." In Scripture, name changes indicate a change in character. In Genesis 32:28, we see the name change of Jacob (swindler) to Israel (one who contends with God). When we enter into covenant relationship, we should evolve and reflect on our new identity as members of the religious community.

During biblical times and now, people in communal societies commonly believed that those entrusted with authority would make decisions that would benefit the community the most. They understood that the action of one affects the lives of many. Abraham's faith affected his future descendants.

God created an *everlasting covenant* with Abraham that is conditional. Its terms extend to Abraham's descendants. In Genesis 17:9, God said to Abraham "As for you, you must keep my covenant, you and your descendants after you for the generations to come." To demonstrate allegiance to covenant, Abraham and all males in his household, blood relatives, slaves, or foreigners, had to be circumcised (Genesis 17:10-14). Circumcision was a condition for inclusion in community.

---

[2] Nick Stinnett, Barbara Chesser, and John DeFrain (Eds.). *Building Family Strengths: Blueprints for Action.* (Lincoln, NE: University of Nebraska Press, 1979), p. 48.

[3] Mendenhall, G. E., & Herion, G. A. (1992). Covenant. In D. N. Freedman (Ed.), *The Anchor Yale Bible Dictionary* (Vol. 1, p. 1179). New York: Doubleday.

[4] Elwell, W. A., & Beitzel, B. J. (1988). Covenant. In *Baker encyclopedia of the Bible* (Vol. 1, p. 531). Grand Rapids, MI: Baker Book House.

CONTEMPORARY COMMUNITY BUILDING:
Pastor Charles Blake and West Angeles Church of God in Christ

Covenant establishes religious community and demands commitment to responsibility and action. The West Angeles Community Development Corporation in Los Angeles, California, reflects this type of commitment. Named among its community services are small business microloans and credit counseling. The Young 'N LA program focuses on mentoring minority men who have been or are currently on probation. The church also offers small-business tax preparation.

In addition, there is a five-week class on entrepreneurship to help people get their business ideas off the ground an eight-hour homebuyer education course, and a home retention clinic for those who have a home and are struggling to make mortgage payments These services promote economic empowerment. Just as many were blessed through Abraham, many families and communities can be blessed through one church or organization.

DISCUSSION

"WHAT" - THE BASICS

1. What does being in covenant with God mean to you?

2. Why is the Abrahamic Covenant so significant? What does it establish?

3. God changed Abram's name to Abraham. How do you believe you would be affected by a name change?

How would you perceive yourself differently?

"SO WHAT" - DIGGING DEEPER

1. Abram's faith was tested during the 25-year span between Genesis 12 and 17. What are some tests you have had that spurred further spiritual growth and maturity in you?

2. The Abrahamic Covenant was conditional. Abraham had an active role to play to reap its benefits. Beyond saying "Yes, Lord," what conditions do you believe Christians must satisfy to be in covenant relationship with Jesus Christ?

3. Abraham's blood relatives, slaves, and foreigners brought into his household were bound by the Abrahamic Covenant. In what ways are your relatives and members of your household bound by your covenant relationship with Jesus Christ? Explain.

4. Through Abraham's covenant relationship with God, we learn that the actions of one affect the lives of many. How do you believe the actions of your church affect the quality of life of others in your family and community? Share examples.

APPLICATION OF SCRIPTURE

"NOW WHAT?" – ACTION STEPS

Personal

There is an ancient prayer practice called the Prayer of Examen. People use it to guide them through a spiritual review of their day with God. The steps are listed below.

1. Become aware of God's presence.

2. Review the day with gratitude.

3. Pay attention to your emotions.

4. Choose one feature of the day and pray from it.

5. Look toward tomorrow.[5]

Take inventory of the kinds of decisions you make regularly. Think about decisions you make about finances, relationships, parenting, employment, education, and faith. List a few of the decisions you have made this week and note the people's lives affected by them. When you get to step four in the Prayer of Examen, focus on one of the decisions you made that involved your family. After praying, reflect on how your covenant relationship with Jesus Christ should influence future decisions you make.

Congregational

Invite your pastor, leaders, and other community-minded people to visit the West Angeles Development Corporation website (www.westangelescdc.org). Notice the types of classes, services, and projects they offer. Brainstorm ways your local church could provide a class or service to develop your community. Even small churches can provide an educational class periodically. Consider inviting people into your facility from the community to educate the public about tax preparation, consumer credit, homeownership, or retirement planning.

MEDITATION

I am connected. We are connected. What I do affects you. What you do affects me. Lord, help me remember that. Remind me that the words I speak and the actions I take can build up or tear down. Remind me that covenant binds me to You and to others. Covenant compels me to do and be what You declare. Show me how to treat You and Your family right.

PRAYER

Dear Lord, through Abraham's story, You call us into covenant again. Lead us through the tests and trials that will build our faith. Help us learn from our mistakes. Keep us humble when we begin "to get it." Help us commit to covenant; not just for ourselves, but also for our families and for our community. Teach us to live as those who live by faith for the glory of God. Amen.

BIBLIOGRAPHY

Elwell, W. A., and Beitzel, B. J. (1988). Covenant. In *Baker Encyclopedia of the Bible* (Vol. 1, p. 531). Grand Rapids, MI: Baker Book House.

---

[5] *The Daily Examen.* www.ignatianspirituality.com. http://www.ignatianspirituality.com/ignatian-prayer/the-examen Retrieved 9/21/2017.

Ignatianspirituality.com *The Daily Examen*. www.ignatianspirituality.com. http://www. ignatianspirituality.com/ignatian-prayer/the-examen Retrieved 9/21/2017.

Krysan, Maria, Kristin A. Moore, and Nicoholas Zill. *Identifying Successful Families: An Overview of Constructs and Selected Measures*. Washington, D.C.: U.S. Department of Health and Human Services, May 10, 1990.

Mendenhall, G. E., & Herion, G. A. (1992). Covenant. In D. N. Freedman (Ed.), *The Anchor Yale Bible Dictionary* (Vol. 1, p. 1179). New York: Doubleday

Stinnett, Nick, Chesser, Barbara, & DeFrain, John (Eds.). *Building family strengths. Blueprints for action*. Lincoln, NE: University of Nebraska Press, 1979.

RECOMMENDED RESOURCES:

West Angeles Community Development Corporation http://www.westangelescdc. org/

NOTES

_____

_____

_____

_____

_____

_____

_____

_____

CHAPTER 4
Skills to Build

Scripture Lesson: Exodus 12:31-35
Background Scriptures: Exodus 12:1-42

MEMORY VERSE

But remember the LORD your God, for it is he who gives you the ability to produce wealth, and so confirms his covenant, which he swore to your ancestors, as it is today. (Deuteronomy 8:18, NIV)

QUESTION

Imagine you lived in 1865. The Civil War just ended. You *have been* enslaved, but now you are free. All your life, others controlled your day. As a newly freed person, what new skills do you believe you need to develop?

INTRODUCTION

African Americans revere the Exodus story of the ancient Israelites. There we meet the God of the oppressed who delivers His people from oppressors. The children of Israel were enslaved during their centuries-long sojourn in Egypt. Only God's might loosened Egypt's oppressive grip on their lives. God used Moses to lead Israel out of bondage. God also sent ten plagues that exposed the Egyptians' gods as frauds. One fateful night, death slew the firstborn of the Egyptians and their livestock, but spared the firstborn of Israel. Wailing filled the air. The once-mighty Egyptians reeled in defeat, while Israel stood ready to act. Fearing total annihilation, Pharaoh sent

Moses and his people away. Israel was free! But a nagging question remained. What do you *do* when you are free for the first time? Israel did not know exactly where to go or how to live outside Egypt. If you were among these newly freed Israelites, what skills would you need to help your family and community?

BLACK HISTORY SPOTLIGHT: Greenwood in Tulsa, Oklahoma

The early African American settlers in Tulsa, Oklahoma, were similar to the Black people who moved to Mound Bayou, Mississippi. These men and women sought opportunities and land to establish a settlement away from the virulent racism of the South. It was not unusual for the early Black residents to have moved several times before coming to Tulsa, a sign that residents were willing to travel long distances to pursue their dreams. O.W. Gurley was probably the first Black to arrive in Tulsa. Born in 1866, Gurley, a son of slaves, grew up in Alabama and later moved to Arkansas. Gurley became a teacher but wanted more for himself and was drawn by the opportunity to acquire land in Oklahoma. He moved to Oklahoma and was part of the land rush of 1893. By 1900, Gurley lived in Perry, Oklahoma, and operated a merchant store.

The discovery of oil in Tulsa provided him with another opportunity for success. Given an opportunity to purchase land on the city's northside, he recognized that the land he purchased could be zoned and sold to Black people. Since the Oklahoma constitution barred all types of racial integration from housing to telephones, Gurley designated the area for African Americans, creating Greenwood.

Gurley took many steps to establish Tulsa as a place of opportunity for African Americans. A keen businessman, he understood that segregation meant that Black people needed a place to live where they could travel to the downtown core to work. He also understood that businesses needed to come to Greenwood if it were to become a sustainable community. But Greenwood was much more than a place where individuals went to make their fortune. What made Greenwood special was the fact that Black people worked together and pooled their resources to build a community.

Greenwood stands today because its residents have always been builders. They used their skills to establish relationships with each other and even outside their communities. Whether it was building organizations, building families, or establishing businesses, Black residents of Tulsa proved adaptable enough to take the necessary risks to adopt successful

strategies that allowed them to seize their dreams. Even the Tulsa race riot of 1921 could not destroy the spirit of a people dedicated to progress and building their community.

SCRIPTURE REFERENCES

(Exodus 12:31-35, NIV)

[31] During the night Pharaoh summoned Moses and Aaron and said, "Up! Leave my people, you and the Israelites! Go, worship the LORD as you have requested. [32] Take your flocks and herds, as you have said, and go. And also bless me." [33] The Egyptians urged the people to hurry and leave the country. "For otherwise," they said, "we will all die!" [34] So the people took their dough before the yeast was added, and carried it on their shoulders in kneading troughs wrapped in clothing. [35] The Israelites did as Moses instructed and asked the Egyptians for articles of silver and gold and for clothing.

LESSON FOCUS

In today's lesson, we enter the Exodus narrative on the night death struck the firstborn of the Egypt's families and livestock. Through these sudden deaths, Egypt experienced God's judgment. Fearful that something worse would befall them, the Egyptians urged Israel's hasty departure. They even doled out articles of silver, gold, and clothing to Israel. (Is this a biblical example of reparations?)

Instantly, Israel's status changed. After hundreds of years of living in Egypt, they were Pharaoh's slave labor no longer. This marked a new beginning for the Israelites.

They were free—physically. The extent of their mental and spiritual freedom remained to be seen. We must wonder if Israel can leave the beliefs and practices of their Egyptian oppressors behind them. The Israelites were free, but what skills did they need to begin anew? This question is the focus of today's lesson.

BIBLE BACKGROUND

The Passover narrative precedes today's passage. The Passover includes a series of strategic acts. First, God tells Moses and Aaron to reset the national calendar. They were to declare the present month (Nissan) the first month of the Hebrew year (Exodus 12:1-2). Second, Israel must take lambs (the Passover lamb) without blemish to kill, eat, and use the blood to paint the doorposts of their houses (Exodus 12:3-8, 21). Israel sacrificed these lambs together, on the same day as a corporate act of faith. This foreshadowed the sacrifice Jesus later made as the Passover Lamb. The Lord's final instructions directed the Israelites to eat the lambs quickly to prepare them for a hasty departure that evening. Though death would strike the Egyptian households, when the Lord saw the lambs' blood on doorposts, death would *pass over* or spare Israel's houses (Exodus 12:11-13). At midnight, the Lord struck down Egypt's firstborn (Exodus 12). To this day, Judaism continues to observe Passover as its most sacred memorial.

Death of their firstborn devastated Egypt. The death of Egypt's firstborn male heirs served judgment on the perpetuation of Egypt's oppressive rule. The death of the firstborn livestock served judgment on the

many Egyptian gods depicted as animals. "During the night Pharaoh summoned Moses and Aaron and said, 'Up! Leave my people, you and the Israelites! Go, worship the LORD as you have requested'" (Exodus 12:31). Fear motivated Pharaoh and the other Egyptians to send the Israelites away.

SCRIPTURE EXPLORATION

Earlier in the Exodus account, Moses and Aaron went to Pharaoh and said, "This is what the Lord, the God of Israel, says: 'Let my people go, so that they may hold a festival to me in the wilderness'" (Exodus 5:1). *Then*, Pharaoh was defiant. In today's passage, Pharaoh quivers in fear. He and all of Egypt had just suffered through ten plagues that demonstrated God's superiority to the Egyptian gods. Pharaoh finally lets Israel go.

God's initial "let my people go" demand centered on worship. Israel was to hold a festival to God *in the wilderness*. The first skill these newly freed Israelites needed was worship to God in the wilderness. This was counterintuitive. The wilderness implies the presence of "wild things" that could do harm. Worship in that context stands in contrast to the normal fight-or-flight stress response we speak about today. Remember, Israel had only known slavery for centuries. They had no allies to protect them outside Egypt's borders.

The Passover meal taught the Israelites a mental skill—readiness. They used unleavened bread and "took their dough before the yeast was added" in their departure (Exodus 12:34). They had to be ready to act decisively at a moment's notice. Readiness requires forethought and planning. One must anticipate future challenges. A readiness mentality prepares you to act quickly when opportunities arise.

Last, the Israelites "asked the Egyptians for articles of silver and gold and for clothing" (Exodus 12:35). This plunder became their start-up or venture capital. This could be considered to be an early example of reparations. The skill the Israelites developed here was financial planning. They needed startup finances to begin their new life.

Of the three skills, the most essential one was learning to worship in the wilderness. After centuries of enslavement, Israel could easily have picked up bad habits like scarcity mentality, acceptance of exploitation, or the urge to control. Observing Pharaoh's constant need to build and hoard could have created similar appetites in the Israelites. Adopting Egyptian ways could perpetuate psychological chains of slavery in Israel's camp long after their physical departure. Israel needed to reestablish its allegiance to God, recommitting to the terms of covenant God made with Abraham.

CONTEMPORARY COMMUNITY BUILDING: Building Our Own Community, Inc.

The Israelites learned new skills upon their exit from Egypt: worship in the wilderness, a readiness mentality, and financial planning. The non-profit agency Building Our Own Community, Inc. (or B.O.O.C., pronounced "book") uses similar skills to restore and strengthen distressed areas. The organization provides activities that develop youth, promotes economic development, and targets health issues in underserved communities. Through its BOOCbotics program, the agency uses robotics to teach youth sportsmanship and leadership skills in science, technology, engineering, and math (STEM). Youth who participate in B.O.O.C. activities are developing a readiness mentality.

DISCUSSION

"WHAT" - THE BASICS

1. In what ways did Israel's participation in Passover activities prepare them for their exodus from Egypt?

2. What divine message did the ten plagues communicate to Pharaoh and Egypt?

3. What message did the tenth plague send to Israel?

"SO WHAT" - DIGGING DEEPER

1. Israel had lived in Egypt for hundreds of years. What harmful habits or attitudes might they have adopted during slavery?

2. What harmful habits or attitudes do you believe African Americans developed during slavery that continue to plague our community today?

3. Identify a "wilderness" facing you today. What would "worshiping in the wilderness" look like in your situation?

4. Which gifts, abilities, and talents do you believe you could use in your wilderness?

APPLICATION OF SCRIPTURE

"NOW WHAT?" – ACTION STEPS

Personal

In today's lesson, God called Israel into the wilderness to worship. The wilderness was an unknown place that offered new possibilities and new challenges. Identify a wilderness opportunity facing you. For example, your wilderness may be a new job prospect, starting a personal business, or organizing a community project. With your wilderness in mind, what would practicing the three skills mentioned in today's lesson (Worship in the wilderness, a readiness mentality, and financial planning) look like for you?

Congregational

Invite your pastor and other church leaders to visit the B.O.O.C. website at www.booc.org. Read about its history and purpose. Note how this church-based organization provides services to develop youth, families, and community. Explore ways to use people's gifts, talents, and abilities to create or partner with existing organizations to help develop your youth, families, and community.

MEDITATION

Free, destiny no longer dictated. Free, no idea how to order my steps. Free, wondering which decision to make. Lord, I'm free from "Pharaoh," now free me from Pharaoh's ways. Show me the skills I need to build my family and my community.

PRAYER

The Lord calls us to worship in the wilderness—the wild places others avoid. We need not be afraid, God tamed Pharaoh. We need not fear, God defeated Egypt's gods. Free our minds, Lord. Free us from old habits that enslave us. Free us from the desire to succeed at the expense of others. Free us to worship you in the wilderness. Through Jesus Christ we pray. Amen.

BIBLIOGRAPHY

Bruggemann, Walter. *Journey to the Common Good*. (Louisville, KY: Westminster John Knox, 2010)

Building Our Own Community BOOC brochure. www.booc.org. Retrieved October 2, 2017. http://www.booc.org/BOOCbotic_Brochure.pdf

Messenger, W. (Ed.). Theology of Work Project. *Genesis through Revelation*. (Vol. 1). (Peabody, MA: Hendrickson Publishers, 2014–2016).

Stuart, D. K. *Exodus* (Vol. 2). (Nashville: Broadman & Holman Publishers, 2006).

RECOMMENDED RESOURCES:

Bruggemann, Walter. *Journey to the Common Good*. (Louisville, KY: Westminster John Knox, 2010)

Building Our Own Community (BOOC) website http://www.booc.org/.

CHAPTER 5

Building God's House

Scripture Lesson: Exodus 25:1-9
Background Scriptures: Exodus 24-25

MEMORY VERSE

Tell the Israelites to bring me an offering. You are to receive the offering for me from everyone whose heart prompts them to give. (Exodus 25:2, NIV)

QUESTION

If you were currently suffering some hardship, which of the following appeals would motivate you to give a financial donation? Explain the reason for your response.

    A. To help the poor

    B. To provide relief following a disaster

    C. To make the community better

    D. To make the world a better place

    E. To help build a sanctuary for your church

INTRODUCTION

In today's passage, the Lord tells the Israelites "take for me an offering" (Exodus 25:2). On the surface this might seem like a strange request to ask formerly enslaved people. For hundreds of years they had few possessions. When leaving captivity, they plundered the Egyptians' silver and gold to provide finances for their exodus. Once freed, the Israelites became nomads. Survival dominated their thoughts—what shall we eat, what shall we drink, where shall we live? They also were a blessed people who God had rescued from Pharaoh's army. God had provided water when they were thirsty and manna when they were hungry. How would these stressed-but-blessed people respond to God's invitation to give? Today's session explores the issues surrounding God's invitation to build God's house.

BLACK HISTORY SPOTLIGHT: Hayti in Durham, North Carolina

Durham's founding was similar to the towns we read of earlier, Mound Bayou and Greenwood. During the Antebellum Period, the southern states lagged behind the northern ones in industrialization. Transportation in the region was often nonexistent. Nevertheless, during the 1850s, some areas in the upper South, including what became Durham, took steps toward industrialization and improving their infrastructure. Bartlett Durham, a large landowner, donated a small piece of his land to the North Carolina Railroad, a railroad that connected North Carolina's coastal plains region with its Piedmont region. Durham Station, the area of his land he donated to the railroad, became one of the station points. In 1869, the General Assembly of North Carolina incorporated the town of Durham.[1]

Durham remained a small town in its formative years. Its lush lands, green scenery, relatively low elevation, and fertile soils made it an attractive migration spot. African Americans came to Durham during these early years. In 1866, a group of Christian African Americans met in the home of Margaret Faucette, an African American woman who was the wife of a local farmer. This group would become the First Missionary Baptist Church, and later, the White Rock Missionary Baptist Church. Services were held on Elm Street and then moved to Fayetteville Street, the center of Hayti.[2]

The lure of jobs and opportunity led to increases in the city's Black population. Between 1890 and 1910, the Black community in Durham rose from 1,859 to 6,869. By 1910, the Black population was approximately 38 percent of the city's population. According to one study, there were at least eleven separate Black communities in Durham, but Hayti was by far the most important and largest. The more prosperous and stable African Americans and their families lived in Hayti, a community that had everything Black people needed to survive on a day-to-day basis. Well-off, single Black women could find a place in Hayti. A prominent resident of Hayti was Fannie Rosser, an employee of the Mutual Insurance Company, who also was a real estate broker and investor.[3]

Hayti continued to thrive through World War II. The community boasted active churches, a movie theater, a hospital, community organizations, such as the YMCA and YWCA, and many Black-owned businesses. For a few years, Hayti was also home to the only Black-owned and -operated textile mill in the country. However, urban renewal and integration helped to destroy much of what Black residents built. By the late 1950s, the city began to demolish many of Hayti's historical buildings. The creation of Interstate 147 further divided the Black community by razing historic landmarks and splitting the community.[4]

Today there is hope for renewal. The Hayti Heritage Center stands on the grounds of the old St. Joseph's Church. Some of the old buildings also remain. There is renewed interest by community leaders rebuild the wonderful community of Hayti. As we learn more about the people of Hayti's past perhaps we will learn more about how people from oppressed spaces

[1] William K. Boyd, *The Story of Durham, City of the New South* (Durham: North Carolina, Duke University Press), 25-8.

[2] "History of White Rock Baptist Church," White Rock Baptist Church, assessed December 5, 2017. http://www.whiterockbaptistchurch.org/history

[3] John N. Ingham, "Building Businesses, Creating Communities: Residential Segregation and the Growth of African American Business in Southern Cities, 1880-1915." *The Business History Review* 77, no. 4 (2003): 660. http://www.jstor.org/stable/30041232; John Kellogg, ""Negro Urban Clusters in the Postbellum South." *Geographical Review* 67, no. 3 (1977): 310-21. doi:10.2307/213725. ; Anne M. Valk and Leslie Brown, *Living with Jim Crow: African American women and memories of the segregated South* (New York: Palgrave Macmillan, 2010), 24

[4] "Digitally Reconstructing Hayti," University of North Carolina, assessed December 5, 2017. http://mainstreet.lib.unc.edu/projects/durham/index.php/markers/view/144

can liberate themselves by building communities of promise.

SCRIPTURE REFERENCES

(Exodus 25:1-9)

¹ The LORD said to Moses, ² "Tell the Israelites to bring me an offering. You are to receive the offering for me from everyone whose heart prompts them to give. ³ These are the offerings you are to receive from them: gold, silver and bronze; ⁴ blue, purple and scarlet yarn and fine linen; goat hair; ⁵ ram skins dyed red and another type of durable leather; acacia wood; ⁶ olive oil for the light; spices for the anointing oil and for the fragrant incense; ⁷ and onyx stones and other gems to be mounted on the ephod and breastpiece. ⁸ "Then have them make a sanctuary for me, and I will dwell among them. ⁹ Make this tabernacle and all its furnishings exactly like the pattern I will show you.

LESSON FOCUS

We meet Israel in survival mode in today's lesson. Their daily routine may have resembled that practiced by people in developing countries today. From sunup to sundown, much of the world spends the day searching for food and water. Many people in the United States live from hand-to-mouth as well. When the pressure to satisfy basic needs consumes people, a divine invitation to give to a building fund might sound unreasonable. Today's lesson thrusts the people of Israel into the challenges surrounding faith formation when they don't have it all together yet. We will take time to explore

the implications of God's invitation to give during uncertain times.

BIBLE BACKGROUND

In session 4, we rehearsed Israel's exodus from Egyptian captivity. As the Hebrews left, they plundered the Egyptians by asking for silver, gold, and clothing (Exodus 12:35-36). These were the few precious possessions Israel had for their journey.

A series of faith-testing experiences followed. Pharaoh pursued Israel, but God delivered them. When there was nothing to drink, God sweetened the waters at Marah. When there was nothing to eat, God rained down manna. God gave Moses the Ten Commandments, and Moses shared them with the people. Each of these events revealed God's providence and care. Nevertheless, the days of everyday survival outnumbered the days of miraculous intervention. Did the burden of survival cause spiritual amnesia in Israel? Does the daily grind of making it ever divert your attention from remembering God's goodness?

In today's passage, Israel is still wandering through the wilderness. Though God is caring for them, Israel encounters other people who worship different gods. Remember, for generations, Israel witnessed the Egyptians worshiping many gods. Did something about these other religions attract Israel? Consider God's actions contained in today's background Bible reading. God summoned Moses to the mountain again where God gave him the Law and instructions for building God a sanctuary. The first of the Ten Commandment declares, "You shall have no other gods before me" (Exodus 20:3). In today's session, we find Moses on the mountain in the midst of receiving instructions from God.

SCRIPTURE EXPLORATION

First, we observe the Lord giving Moses instructions to Israel. "Bring me an offering . . . receive [it] from everyone whose heart prompts them to give" (Exodus 25:2). The Hebrew rendering of this verse reads, "every man 'whose heart makes him vow," in short, this person desires to give.[5] Jesus echoes this thought in the Sermon on the Mount, "For where your treasure is, there your heart will be also" (Matthew 6:21). God invites us to share voluntarily; we see no strong-arm, guilt-inducing tactics here.

Exodus 25 includes a precise list of items God desired to create the sacred dwelling. The precious metals and fine linen appear early in the list. They were items the Israelites had in their possession since plundering the Egyptians. How challenging this must have been for the Israelites to think of giving away some of their few valuables. How many meals might gold earrings buy? This points out the sacrificial nature of giving to God.

The linen, animal skins, acacia wood, oils, spices, and stones were offerings the people could have provided through skilled labor. Fine linen translated from *šēš*, an Egyptian word, referred to linen made of threads twisted from many strands. It's likely that the Israelites learned how to make Egyptian linen during their captivity.[6] The other materials, mainly wood, were available locally. Individuals could have labored and given their time and talent to craft these materials.

The sanctuary was actually the Tabernacle; a portable tent. It was a *tent of dwelling* where God's presence resided, and a *tent of meeting* where God communicated as law-giver, judge, and guide.[7] The Tabernacle had an inner shrine (the 'Holy of Holies') that housed the Ark of the Covenant, and an outer chamber (the 'Holy Place') that contained the seven-branched lampstand, the table for the bread of presence, and the altar of incense. The Tabernacle was a reminder of God's continual presence. The Tabernacle was portable, and could be dismantled and reassembled whenever Israel moved. It became the focal point of the Israelite community. The twelve tribes situated themselves around the Tabernacle when they camped. This sacred place provided a visual reminder of God's relationship with them. One aspect of this relationship was complete obedience. The Tabernacle created a designated location for Israel to worship God in the wilderness.

The detailed instructions reflected God's demand for strict adherence to God's Word. There is no ambiguity in intent. Exodus 25:9 makes this clear: "Make this tabernacle and all its furnishings exactly like the pattern I will show you." Worship in

[5] Cole, R. A. (1973). *Exodus: an introduction and commentary* (Vol. 2, p. 197). Downers Grove, IL: InterVarsity Press.

[6] Hannah, J. D. (1985). Exodus. In J. F. Walvoord & R. B. Zuck (Eds.), *The Bible Knowledge Commentary: An Exposition of the Scriptures* (Vol. 1, pp. 147–148). Wheaton, IL: Victor Books.

[7] Hyun, T. (2016). Tabernacle. In J. D. Barry, D. Bomar, D. R. Brown, R. Klippenstein, D. Mangum, C. Sinclair Wolcott, ... W. Widder (Eds.), *The Lexham Bible Dictionary*. Bellingham, WA: Lexham Press.

the wilderness was a primary reason God delivered Israel from Egyptian captivity. Remember the following statement from Session 4? "God's initial 'Let my people go' demand [to Pharaoh] centered on worship. Israel was to hold a festival to God in the wilderness." God dwelling in the Tabernacle in Exodus foreshadows God dwelling within us mentioned in Revelation.

"And I heard a loud voice from the throne saying, 'Now the dwelling of God is with men, and he will live with them. They will be his people, and God himself will be with them and be their God.' " (Revelation 21:3)

COMMUNITY DEVELOPMENT BUILDING:
St. Paul's Missionary Baptist Church Family Life Center

In today's passage, the Tabernacle was the place where God dwelled and communicated with Israel. As Christians, God dwells within us and speaks directly to us. The Apostle Paul says, "Do you not know that your bodies are temples of the Holy Spirit, who is in you, whom you have received from God? You are not your own" (1 Corinthians 6:19). St. Paul Missionary Baptist Church in Sacramento, California, took this passage to heart and created a ministry to develop these temples of the Holy Spirit. This church constructed a family life center, "dedicated to promoting physical fitness, proper nutrition, recreation, health, and wellness."[8] Their program offerings include fitness classes, youth summer camps, and adult volleyball, basketball, and racquetball leagues. The affordable memberships are open to members of the church and the public.

DISCUSSION

"WHAT" - THE BASICS

1. Were you ever asked to make a donation that caused your head (logic) to argue with you heart (compassion)? What was the outcome?

2. The Tabernacle was a visual reminder of God's presence. What reminds you of God's presence daily? How does that reminder influence your actions?

3. Why do you believe God asked for offerings from people whose heart prompted them to give? What purpose would that serve?

4. How was carrying out God's precise instructions for building the sanctuary a spiritual exercise?

"SO WHAT" - DIGGING DEEPER

1. Why do you believe God asked Israel to give precious items to build the sanctuary?

2. God had spoken through Moses to deliver Israel from Egypt and to care for them in the wilderness. Why do you believe God now instructed Israel to build God a sanctuary?

3. In what ways do you believe seeing the Tabernacle daily influenced Israel?

---

[8] Stpaulsac.org. "Dr. Ephraim Williams Family Life Center." http://stpaulsac.org/family-life-center/ Retrieved October 14, 2017.

APPLICATION OF SCRIPTURE

"NOW WHAT?" – ACTION STEPS

Personal

The first of God's Ten Commandments says "I am the LORD your God, who brought you out of Egypt, out of the land of slavery. You shall have no other gods before me" (Exodus 20:2-3). Israel had heard this before Moses went to the mountain where he received the instructions for building the sanctuary for God. Within this commandment is a reminder, God brought Israel out of Egypt and slavery. For what are you thankful to God? Create a list of milestone events for which you give thanks to God. How might you say "thank you" to God through your time, talent, and treasure? Write a list of concrete examples. Pledge to do one of the items on the list within the next two weeks.

Congregational

A recent report from the National Center for Health Statistics states that nearly 40 percent of Americans are obese.[9] This leads to a host of illness and disease that is entirely preventable. This is not a good way to steward our bodies, which are the temples of the Holy Spirit. Brainstorm ways to promote greater physical fitness among your church members and people from your surrounding community. Topics may include better nutrition (consider introducing healthy snacks at church functions); health screenings (invite representatives from local health agencies to do free screenings); physical fitness (start a fitness club—make individual challenges to walk or run together.) Provide public encouragement for participation during worship. Brainstorm additional ideas with interested parties.

MEDITATION

Too often I feel stretched beyond capacity. My family wants this, my job wants that, and I'm not sure *which* bill I can afford to pay next. Lord, when I hear You say *give*, sometimes I want to scream *how*? Free me from the tyranny of my narrow world. Teach me to trust You when I'm in the wilderness. Show me *how* to give. Lord, show me how to refocus my attention on You.

PRAYER

Dear Lord, ask my heart to give, though my head may argue. Ask my hands to share what I'd rather keep. Teach me to say thank you while I wander in the wilderness. Amen.

BIBLIOGRAPHY

Cole, R. A. *Exodus: An Introduction and Commentary* (Vol. 2, p. 197). (Downers Grove, IL: InterVarsity Press, 1973)

Hannah, J. D. Exodus in J. F. Walvoord & R. B. Zuck (Eds.), *The Bible Knowledge Commentary: An Exposition of the Scriptures* (Vol. 1, pp. 147–148). (Wheaton, IL: Victor Books, 1985)

---

[9] Sifferlin, Alexandra. "40% of Americans Are Obese—And the Trend Isn't Slowing" http://time.com/4980225/obesity-rates-adults-children/ (Accessed October 23, 2017)

Hyun, T. Tabernacle in J. D. Barry, D. Bomar, D. R. Brown, R. Klippenstein, D. Mangum, C. Sinclair Wolcott, … W. Widder (Eds.), *The Lexham Bible Dictionary*. (Bellingham, WA: Lexham Press, 2016).

Stpaulsac.org. "Dr. Ephraim Williams Family Life Center." http://stpaulsac.org/family-life-center/ Retrieved October 14, 2017.

RECOMMENDED RESOURCES:

Rockridge Press. *Juicing for Beginners: The Essential Guide to Juicing Recipes and Juicing for Weight Loss*. (Berkeley, CA: Rockridge Press, 2013)

Smith, Ian K. *Eat: Feed Your Body and Starve the Fat*. (New York, NY: St. Martin's Press, 2011)

St. Paul Missionary Baptist Church Family Life Center http://stpaulsac.org/family-life-center/

NOTES

_____

_____

_____

_____

_____

_____

_____

_____

_____

_____

CHAPTER 6
Moses Builds Leaders

Scripture Lesson: Exodus 18:21-24
Background Scriptures: Exodus 18

> **MEMORY VERSE**
> *Pursue righteousness, godliness, faith, love, endurance and gentleness.*
> (1 Timothy 6:11b, NIV)

QUESTION

Imagine people want to choose leaders to improve living conditions in your neighborhood (for example: provide affordable homes to own, clean up vacant lots, build grocery stores, etc.). Which character traits and skills would you want these leaders to possess? Share the reasons for your choices.

INTRODUCTION

Have you ever watched people choose poor leaders and wonder why people don't know how to choose good leaders? If so, you are not alone. This scenario plays itself out regularly in business, politics, and churches. Much of what is written about how to choose good leaders comes out of the business community.

Jeffrey Cohn, CEO advisor and coach, says we look at the wrong things when choosing leaders, "like a candidate's charm, their stellar résumé, or their academic credentials."[1] People erroneously use the following phrase as their litmus test: "the best predictor of future behavior is past behavior."[2] In reality, the business community recommends other leadership qualifiers—beginning with good character traits. Look for "integrity, passion, courage, vision, judgment, empathy, and emotional intelligence,"[3] says Cohn. Business thinker and author Erika Andersen suggests asking questions like these: "Does the person fit the business?" "Is the person open to learning?" "Is he or she 'followable'?"[4]

Today's lesson invites us to think about how we should choose our leaders and

---

[1] Cohn, Jeffrey. "Why we pick bad leaders and how to spot the good ones." http://www.cnn.com http://www.cnn.com/2012/02/14/opinion/cohn-pick-leaders/index.html (accessed October 16, 2017).

[2] Franklin, Karen. "The best predictor of future behavior is . . . past behavior." Does the popular maxim hold water? www.psychologytoday.com. https://www.psychologytoday.com/blog/witness/201301/the-best-predictor-future-behavior-is-past-behavior Retrieved October 16, 2017.

[3] Cohn, Jeffrey. "Why we pick bad leaders and how to spot the good ones." http://www.cnn.com http://www.cnn.com/2012/02/14/opinion/cohn-pick-leaders/index.html (accessed October 16, 2017).

[4] Franklin, Karen. "The best predictor of future behavior is . . . past behavior." Does the popular maxim hold water? www.psychologytoday.com. https://www.psychologytoday.com/blog/witness/201301/the-best-predictor-future-behavior-is-past-behavior Retrieved October 16, 2017.

what process we should use to identify people who can lead us effectively at church, work, and in the community.

BLACK HISTORY SPOTLIGHT:
Eatonville, Florida

In 1935, Alan Lomax, a renowned musicologist and folklorist, travelled to Florida with scholars Zora Neale Hurston and Mary Elizabeth Barnicle to study the African Americans who lived there. Lomax's working relationship with Hurston, who grew up in Eatonville, surely helped him gain the trust of the local residents. On June 22, after collecting oral histories from the local residents, Lomax sat down to write a letter addressed to his family. In his letter, he wrote about the distinctiveness of Eatonville as a Black town, noting that "the white people of this part of the country have left them to themselves pretty much for the last fifty years."

Even today, Eatonville remains a curiosity. Although there were a number of Black towns and settlements throughout the United States in the years after Reconstruction, not all of them were incorporated. An incorporated town is a municipality that has received recognition from the state to elect its own town government. As an incorporated town, residents of Eatonville elected their own officers and selected their police without intrusion. As a people coming out of slavery and Reconstruction, the psychological impact and privilege of seeing African Americans effectively manage their livelihoods instilled in Hurston and other residents the importance of Black independence and self-determination.

Eatonville's promise of an oasis from racism and the opportunity to establish a new life brought people to the town. Eatonville was a place where Black people could establish themselves. Hurston writes about her parents, "So these two began their new life. Both of them swore that things were going to be better, and it came to pass as they said. They bought land, built a roomy house, planted their acres and reaped."[5]

Today Eatonville is experiencing a revival, just as its most well-known resident's legacy continues to grow. Although relatively forgotten after her death in 1960, by the 1980s, Hurston's work, particularly her best work, *Their Eyes Were Watching God*, had become a part of America's literary canon. Meanwhile, Eatonville continues to battle ongoing issues. This includes a high poverty level that remains twice the national level. This is reflective a reality across the United States, as African American unemployment is approximately twice the rate of White Americans. Nevertheless, the spirit of Black self-governance and progress remains strong in Eatonville. In the late 1980s, the county wanted to put a highway through the middle of the town. In protest, residents responded by organizing the Zora Neale Hurston Festival. Thousands came from everywhere to support the festival and the town. Eatonville was resilient and the county gave up the road project. Each year people return to Eatonville for the Zora Neale Hurston Festival. The town remains a curiosity, but its residents continue to see the value in their community that Zora

---

[5] Hurston, *Dust Tracks*, 10

saw. They stand on the foundational pillars of Eatonville: the church, the school, and the family.

SCRIPTURE REFERENCES

(Exodus 18:21-24, NIV)

21 But select capable men from all the people—men who fear God, trustworthy men who hate dishonest gain—and appoint them as officials over thousands, hundreds, fifties and tens. 22 Have them serve as judges for the people at all times, but have them bring every difficult case to you; the simple cases they can decide themselves. That will make your load lighter, because they will share it with you. 23 If you do this and God so commands, you will be able to stand the strain, and all these people will go home satisfied." 24 Moses listened to his father-in-law and did everything he said.

LESSON FOCUS

As we join today's biblical narrative, Moses and Aaron have been carrying most of the leadership burden for Israel. They led the Hebrews out of captivity. They guided them through the wilderness. The all-consuming responsibility must have weighed heavily upon them. For Moses, the primary spokesperson for God, the burden was even greater. God only summoned him for divine instruction on Mt. Sinai. He alone bore the responsibility for sharing what God said, but was he called to lead alone? Sometimes when leaders invest in their work so heavily, they try to do too much. Jethro's statement to Moses emphasizes this point: "The work is too heavy for you; you cannot handle it alone" (Exodus 18:18).

When leaders are too heavily invested, they can begin to assume the success of the business, the family, or the church depends entirely on them. Leading then becomes a lonely, exclusive exercise that exhausts the leader and burdens the people. Thankfully, God often sends a voice of reason to such leaders. In today's passage, Jethro is that voice. He offers Moses reasoned advice. He advises Moses on how to lead, and how to choose and develop good leaders.

BIBLE BACKGROUND

In today's lesson, we find Moses getting a visit from his father-in-law, Jethro. Jethro was a priest of Midian, yet his exact religious affiliation is a matter of debate among scholars. Some believe he worshiped a tribal god named Yahweh, which was not the same as Israel's God, Yahweh. The single point of agreement among scholars is that Jethro was a god-fearing and god-serving man. After hearing Moses rehearse the deeds God performed to set Israel free, Jethro declared, "Now I know that the LORD is greater than all other gods . . . " (Exodus 18:11). This indicates that Jethro became convinced of God's greatness after hearing how God delivered Israel from captivity. That acknowledgment made Jethro unique among other Midianites, who were thought to be idolaters.

Today's passage is a dialog between Moses and Jethro. Jethro saw that Moses was assuming too much responsibility. He offered advice Moses could hear because they had a good relationship.

"What you are doing is not good." Jethro cared about Moses and the people.

"You will only wear yourselves out." He recommended revisiting Moses' job description.

"You must be the people's representative before God." He told Moses to provide spiritual instruction,

"Teach them [God's] decrees and instructions." He urged intentional character development,

"Show them the way they are to live and how to behave" (Exodus 18:17-20). In short, Jethro gave Moses a plan to choose and to develop leaders for Israel's judicial system.

SCRIPTURE EXPLORATION

Jethro's suggestions to develop leaders for Israel's judicial system were extraordinary. Unlike the Israelite priesthood or the monarchy of surrounding tribes, these leaders were to be appointed on the basis of honesty and ability" rather than an assumed hereditary rite. Nepotism (favoritism based on kinship) was not to be part of this system.

Jethro then provided character requirements for those appointed to leadership. Here is the list: (1) Capable— this indicates the candidates had demonstrated ability; (2) Fear God—only those who respected God were suitable; (3) Trustworthy, hating dishonest gain—these traits highlight integrity; leaders should not let money or personal favor sway them.

Last, Jethro recommended a way to order the work, "appoint them as officials over thousands, hundreds, fifties and tens" (Exodus 18:21b). This advice brought peace and spread the responsibility for

justice throughout the community. In effect, Jethro helped decentralize power in Israel and encouraged shared governance. Thankfully, Moses heeded the advice and implemented each recommendation his father-in-law gave him.

CONTEMPORARY COMMUNITY BUILDING: African American Clergy and Political Action

Moses implemented Jethro's recommendations, which helped bring remedies to some of Israel's governing problems. We still need wise advocates for our communities. Some choose to advocate through political means. Historically, some African American clergy have participated in politics to bring just solutions to community problems. A short list includes Adam Clayton Powell Jr., Andrew Young, Walter Fauntroy, Emanuel Cleaver, Clementa Pinckney, and James Meeks. Former Senator Meeks led the "Dry Up" protest to close 26 liquor stores in Roseland, a community on Chicago's South Side, and he sponsored a bill to address critical issues regarding low-income housing. Today's lesson highlights the continual need to develop leaders able to govern justly at all levels of society.

DISCUSSION

"WHAT" - THE BASICS

1. What motivated Jethro to offer leadership advice to Moses?

2. Why do you believe Moses tried to shoulder so much leadership responsibility? What can you

learn about leadership from your conclusions?

3. What leadership lessons can we learn from Jethro's advice?

"SO WHAT" - DIGGING DEEPER

1. What were the major action steps in Jethro's recommendations to Moses? Which of Jethro's recommendations does your local church use to develop leaders?

2. Which character traits did Jethro state potential leaders needed to demonstrate? Think of a specific leadership position in your local church. Which character traits would a person need to demonstrate to be considered for leadership for that position?

3. In today's passage, people waited in line from morning until evening to get a hearing about their concerns. In addition to waiting for justice, what do you believe people can or should do to address their concerns?

APPLICATION OF SCRIPTURE

"NOW WHAT?" – ACTION STEPS

Personal

Reflect on the following:

Today's passage reveals three characters: Jethro, the wise sage offering helpful advice; Moses, the overburdened leader drowning in work; and the people waiting in long lines for justice. Which of these characters do you most identify with today? After reflecting on this passage and your identification with one of the characters, what do you believe God is saying to do, be, or change? To whom should you be listening for advice? To whom should you be offering advice?

Congregational

Brainstorm responses to the following question:

Jethro outlined a leadership development process. If you were to design an intentional leadership development process for leaders in your local church, what would you include?

MEDITATION

Good leaders express concern for others. Seasoned leaders develop relationships through which they can offer advice to other leaders. Spiritual leaders develop people of character who can become leaders. Godly leaders share rather than horde power and authority. Lord, we *know* these things. Show us how to *do* them.

PRAYER

Dear Lord, when I need to be someone's Jethro, I will speak. When I am overburdened, like Moses, I will listen. When I join the long line awaiting justice, I will do what I can to help. Help each of us take what we have learned and put it into practice. Amen.

BIBLIOGRAPHY

Cohn, Jeffrey. "Why we pick bad leaders and how to spot the good ones."

http://www.cnn.com http://www.cnn.com/2012/02/14/opinion/cohn-pick-leaders/index.html (accessed October 16, 2017).

Franklin, Karen. "The best predictor of future behavior is . . . past behavior." Does the popular maxim hold water? www.psychologytoday.com. https://www.psychologytoday.com/blog/witness/201301/the-best-predictor-future-behavior-is-past-behavior Retrieved October 16, 2017.

Slayton, J. C. *Jethro (Person)*. In D. N. Freedman (Ed.), *The Anchor Yale Bible Dictionary* (Vol. 3, p. 821). New York: Doubleday, 1992.

Stuart, D. K. *Exodus* (Vol. 2). Nashville: Broadman & Holman Publishers, 2006.

RECOMMENDED RESOURCES:

Blanchard, Ken, Phil Hodges, & Phyllis Hendry. *Lead Like Jesus Revisited*. Nashville: W Publishing, an imprint of Thomas Nelson, 2016.

Clinton, Robert. *The Making of a Leader: Recognizing the Lessons and Stages of Leadership Development* (Revised and Updated). Colorado Springs, CO: NavPress, 2012.

Friedman, Edward H. *A Failure of Nerve, Revised Edition: Leadership in the Age of the Quick Fix*. New York, NY: Church Publishing, 2017.

NOTES

_____

_____

_____

_____

_____

_____

_____

CHAPTER 7
Building Within Boundaries

Scripture Lesson: Deuteronomy 4:5-8

Background Scriptures: Exodus 20:1-21; Deuteronomy 1:3, 3:28, 4:1-20

> ## MEMORY VERSE
> *Jesus replied: "'Love the Lord your God with all your heart and with all your soul and with all your mind.'"* (Matthew 22:37, NIV)

QUESTION

The Merriam-Webster Dictionary defines the term "litmus test" as "a test in which a single factor (such as an attitude, event, or fact) is decisive." If you lived during the time of Moses, what litmus test do you believe would be used to determine whether you belonged to the people of God?

INTRODUCTION

The histories of the Israelites and African Americans share common themes. Like the Israelites, African Americans suffered in bondage for many generations. Both groups had to learn how to live as free people after their emancipation. Like the Israelites, African Americans had to create community in the midst of hostile peoples. For Israel, surrounding nations and their idolatrous belief systems threatened her potential to create godly communities. Similarly, African Americans faced hostilities from much of the population and the United States government. Houston Hartsfield Holloway, an African American freedman, aptly described the post-slavery

dilemma: "We colored people did not know how to be free and the white people did not know how to have a free colored person about them."[1]

The U.S. government established Black Codes that granted certain legal rights enabling Blacks to marry, and to own property. Those same codes prevented Blacks from serving on juries, testifying against Whites, or serving in state militias. The Black Codes required Black sharecroppers to sign labor contracts with White landowners or face arrest.[2]

Many African Americans turned to Black churches as a major source for spiritual renewal and inspiration. These congregations became centers for community organization. A quote from a 1758 registry says this about the Black church, "This institution which was the

---

[1] Civil War and Reconstruction, 1861-1877: The Freedmen. The Library of Congress. http://loc.gov/teachers/classroommaterials/presentationsandactivities/presentations/timeline/civilwar/freedmen/ Retrieved November 3, 2017

[2] "Life after slavery for African Americans." www.khanacademy.org. https://www.khanacademy.org/humanities/ap-us-history/period-5/apush-reconstruction/a/life-after-slavery Retrieved November 3, 2017.

first source of land ownership for slaves in America (with the human character of Black people) is viewed as the reason and savior of oppressed African people in the United States."[3] Clearly, the influence of the Christian faith shaped the moral fiber of many African Americans who established Black communities and institutions.

Today's Bible lesson occurs 40 years after Israel's exodus from Egypt; an entire generation has died wandering in the wilderness. We observe the children of Israel learning what it meant to be free. While Israel had left Egypt physically, remnants of Egypt, its religious system, and way of life remained in the collective memory of Israel. In addition, the influence of surrounding nations threatened to lure Israel into ungodly religious and social practices. Israel needed to write a new script for life. God's decrees and laws provided the moral framework for that script.

BLACK HISTORY SPOTLIGHT:
Jackson Ward in Richmond, Virginia

In many ways, African American history is analogous to the Israelite sojourn to the Promised Land. In both cases, prejudice kept the communities from many things. Yet, even within the restraints, God provided ways for His people to build a community. This was the case with Jackson Ward in Richmond, Virginia. African Americans did not create Jackson Ward; it was a political construct from the Reconstruction period. Richmond's city council gerrymandered the northern portions of Richmond City into a predominately Black district. In creating this district of mostly African Americans, the conservatives on Richmond's city council gave Blacks control over one district while blocking Blacks from control in the other five districts.

Jackson Ward was much more, however, than simply a political conspiracy to suppress Black votes. The established district did not restrict Black participation in social or business endeavors. People like Maggie Lena Walker, who lived in Jackson Ward, bypassed other churches in the ward to attend the First Baptist Church a few miles away. Other Blacks who lived right outside Jackson Ward conducted their business in the ward.[4]

Even though Black Richmonders found themselves limited from the larger political arena, Blacks who lived in Jackson Ward and its immediate outskirts prospered economically and socially. Through networks of communication and association, Black Richmonders pooled their resources to create a sustainable community.

Many Black Richmonders did very well individually in their businesses, and together, they demonstrated a desire to give back to their community through their churches and fraternal organizations. They took pride in these organizations and worked hard through them to provide opportunity for other residents. Black church leaders played a central role in bringing the community together.

[3] "The Black Church," A Brief History. www.aaregistry.org http://www.aaregistry.org/historic_events/view/black-church-brief-history Retrieved November 3, 2017.

[4] M.M. Branch, "Maggie Lena Walker," The Encyclopedia of Virginia, www. EncyclopediaVirginia.org/Maggie_Lena_Walker_1864-1934 (assessed December 7, 2017)

By 1920, Black residents in Jackson Ward had created a community that provided almost every service and occupation that could be expected. The district served as a local hot spot for the most prominent Black entertainers, and even boasted its own Black art gallery. There was a great focus on building up the youth community; churches and fraternal organizations provided entertainment for youth; several large athletic clubs mentored young Black Richmonders. There was a very strong YMCA and YWCA in the community.

The challenges for Jackson Ward, however, emerged around the time of World War I. In a similar trajectory to Mound Bayou, the community suffered tremendous population losses as Black residents moved North. *The Richmond Planet* certainly recognized the possibility of population decline in 1918 when it began printing stories about the migration in a more negative light. In one article, it stated that the high cost of living nullifies the decent salaries offered in the North. Another piece reported, "in the north the colored citizen is being regarded as an interloper and outside the pale of law." Even though the editors of *The Richmond Planet* were careful to not openly criticize the migration, they certainly seemed to have been concerned about the potential implications of such migration. Nevertheless, the migration would continue, and increased even more during the depression and World War II. The migration continued when an interstate highway split the community. Homeownership dropped and tenancy increased as Black people moved outside the traditional Black neighborhoods and into the suburbs by the late twentieth century.[5]

Even though Jackson Ward has not yet recovered its once privileged status, it is going through a renaissance today. It is now a National Historic District filled with museums, art spaces, and historical landmarks dedicated to the African American experience. Jackson Ward is alive once more.

SCRIPTURE REFERENCES

(Deuteronomy 4:5-8)

[5] See, I have taught you decrees and laws as the LORD my God commanded me, so that you may follow them in the land you are entering to take possession of it. [6] Observe them carefully, for this will show your wisdom and understanding to the nations, who will hear about all these decrees and say, "Surely this great nation is a wise and understanding people." [7] What other nation is so great as to have their gods near them the way the LORD our God is near us whenever we pray to him? [8] And what other nation is so great as to have such righteous decrees and laws as this body of laws I am setting before you today?

LESSON FOCUS

Today's passage examines Israel near the end of its 40-year journey of wandering in the wilderness. The time has come for the people to settle permanently in one place. God again uses Moses to communicate God's terms for living. The decrees and

---

[5] *Richmond Planet,* Jan 5, 1918

laws God gives will provide Israel with wisdom to establish a caring community. Obeying God's decrees will distinguish Israel from other nations. Israel will be known as a wise and discerning nation.

BIBLE BACKGROUND

In today's background reading from Deuteronomy 4, Moses urged Israel to heed and obey God's decrees and laws in preparation for establishing a permanent community in the Promised Land. He reminded the Israelites that they had tried doing things their way at Baal Peor and God punished them for it. Through that event, Israel learned that the only way to survive in the new land was through faithful obedience to God's covenant and laws.

In light of that, Moses then says to Israel, "See, I have taught you decrees and laws as the LORD my God commanded me, so that you may follow them in the land you are entering to take possession of it" (Deuteronomy 4:5).

The term "decree" carries various meanings. In the ancient world, decrees usually appeared in written form. Human rulers and authority figures pronounced decrees (orders) to direct people's conduct, especially in significant matters for communities or individuals.[6] God also issued decrees. Divine decrees often spoke of God's eternal wisdom and plan for creation. Israel would need divine wisdom and a plan for creating community in their new land.

[6] Efird, J. M. (2011). Decrees. In M. A. Powell (Ed.), *The HarperCollins Bible Dictionary (Revised and Updated)* (Third Edition, p. 190). New York: HarperCollins.

SCRIPTURE EXPLORATION

Today's Scripture begins with the word, "See." It is a call to attention. Moses is appealing to Israel's memory. "See, I have taught you decrees" (from Deuteronomy 4:5). Chief among these decrees is the Ten Commandments God gave at Mount Sinai (Exodus 20:1-21). These commandments outline how one should relate to God and neighbor. Israel must learn how to create community, i.e. God's commonwealth. This quest, in the words of Walter Brueggemann, is the journey to the common good.

Israel had been following the script written for them by Egypt for 430 years. The Egyptian script etched exploitation and lust for possessions in Israel's memory. Enslavement can cause psychological trauma, and can express itself through the oppressed becoming grateful for their dependent status. Israel showed evidence of such trauma. The people complained about their emancipation and wished to be in the hands of their captors again. "If only we had died by the LORD's hand in Egypt! There we sat around pots of meat and ate all the food we wanted" (from Exodus 16:3). And, "We remember the fish we ate in Egypt at no cost—also the cucumbers, melons, leeks, onions and garlic" (Numbers 11:5). The mere thought of Egyptian food erased the memory of the Egyptian lash. The Israelites needed to learn a new way of thinking about themselves and about God.

The Ten Commandments (the primary set of decrees issued to Israel) began reshaping how Israel imagined themselves and God. Several of the commandments illustrate this point. The first commandment reminded Israel that God brought them out of Egypt and slavery. It is only this God, the One who overcame Egypt's gods and oppressive work culture, that Israel should worship. The first commandment prompts Israel to declare God as supreme.

To ensure Israel focused on God alone, the second commandment forbade them from making any graven images of other gods. God tolerates no people distracted by false promises from lesser gods. The fourth commandment, honoring the Sabbath, provides a reasonable order for the work week in the community. Sabbath keeping is more than physical rest from labor. It includes being mindful of who God is, what God does, and what it means to be God's people. We experience these actions when we worship God on the Sabbath. Being mindful of God is the first step toward moral character development.

Commandments six through ten teach us how to live peaceably and ethically with each other. In short, they promote respect for others and their possessions, and demand honest speech. Taken together, these decrees provided the basis for establishing good human relations and community, and meaningful worship of God. By obeying these and other decrees from God, Israel will gain wisdom and develop loving compassion toward others. The fruit borne from obeying these decrees will demonstrate the righteousness of God's commandments. The surrounding nations will regard Israel as a "wise and understanding people."

During her wilderness journey, Israel received decrees from God like the following: "If anyone is poor among your fellow Israelites in any of the towns of the land the LORD your God is giving you, do not be hardhearted or tightfisted toward them. Rather, be openhanded and freely lend them whatever they need" (Deuteronomy 15:7-8). These decrees shaped the community's morality and cultivated charitable behavior toward others.

CONTEMPORARY COMMUNITY BUILDING: Bishop Jerry W. Macklin and Glad Tidings Church Of God In Christ

Bishop Jerry W. Macklin is the founding pastor of Glad Tidings Church Of God In Christ in Hayward, California. The church is making an impact in the Northern California community in various ways. One of its major ministry arms is the Northern California Community Development Corporation. The corporation focuses on economic development, housing, education, and community policing. Through the efforts of Bishop Macklin and the community development corporation, the South Hayward neighborhood has experienced a major revitalization.

DISCUSSION

"WHAT" - THE BASICS

1. In what ways does Israel's wilderness story mirror the post-slavery story of African Americans? Name some of the similar challenges faced by the newly freed Israelites and the newly freed African Americans.

2. Why do you believe Israel needed to heed God's decrees in preparation for establishing a permanent community in the Promised Land?

3. In what ways do you believe obeying God's decrees (like the Ten Commandments) distinguished Israel from neighboring nations? Give examples.

"SO WHAT" - DIGGING DEEPER

1. In what ways did Israel's memory of Pharaoh and Egyptian oppression continue to cause Israel problems?

2. Read Exodus 20:1-6. Why do you believe God needed to spend time reminding Israel about their deliverance by God's hand? What things has God done for you that you need to remember to reaffirm your faith?

3. In what ways do you believe remembering God's words and deeds helped strengthen community in Israel?

4. How does remembering God's words and deeds strengthen your church community? Share specific examples.

APPLICATION OF SCRIPTURE

"NOW WHAT?" – ACTION STEPS

Personal

Meditate on the Ten Commandments located in Exodus 20:1-21. Think about the morals these commandments are designed to instill. Which of the commandments is speaking the loudest to you today? After reflecting on the "loudest commandment," what do you believe God is asking you to do, be, or change? Write down your thoughts and act on the action you indicated.

Congregational

Corporations often find ways to be socially responsible in the neighborhood in which the business is located. Consider gathering leaders from local churches and as well as the local business community to talk about how you might work together to build your community. This may involve working on a common cause such as increasing affordable housing, or job creation for youth. Consult other community-based organizations and identify causes that your church or a group of churches could work on collectively.

MEDITATION

Israel wandered for 40 years clutching Egypt's memory to her bosom. Do we ever do the same? Are we in some wilderness, slogging under the weight of the past? Do we waste time searching for something resembling the bad situation we just left? Come see about us, Lord. Don't let us wallow in the past. Remind us again of Your will and Your way that leads us to the right path.

PRAYER

Lord, show us how to be in community. For too long, we've spent time chasing idols of selfishness. Teach us how to love each other as Christ loves the Church. Remind us daily that our neighbors outside the church building need Your love. May we not overlook a single opportunity to bless others as You have blessed us. Amen.

BIBLIOGRAPHY

Brueggemann, Walter. *Journey to the Common Good*. Louisville: Westminster John Knox, 2010.

Brueggemann, Walter. *Sabbath as Resistance: Saying No to the Culture of Now*. Louisville: Westminster John Knox, 2014.

Civil War and Reconstruction, 1861-1877: The Freedmen. The Library of Congress. http://loc.gov/teachers/classroommaterials/presentationsandactivities/presentations/timeline/civilwar/freedmen/ Retrieved November 3, 2017

Efird, J. M. (2011). Decrees. In M. A. Powell (Ed.), *The HarperCollins Bible Dictionary (Revised and Updated)* (Third Edition, p. 190). New York: HarperCollins.

"Life after slavery for African Americans." www.khanacademy.org. https://www.khanacademy.org/humanities/ap-us-history/period-5/apush-reconstruction/a/life-after-slavery Retrieved November 3, 2017.

"The Black Church," A Brief History. www.aaregistry.org http://www.aaregistry.org/historic_events/view/black-church-brief-history Retrieved November 3, 2017.

RECOMMENDED RESOURCES:

Brueggemann, Walter. *Journey to the Common Good*. Louisville: Westminster John Knox, 2010.

Brueggemann, Walter. *Sabbath as Resistance: Saying No to the Culture of Now*. Louisville: Westminster John Knox, 2014.

NOTES

_____

_____

_____

_____

_____

CHAPTER 8

Joshua's Building Blocks

Scripture Lesson: Joshua 4:1-7; Deuteronomy 6:7
Background Scriptures: Joshua 3; Deuteronomy 6:4-9

MEMORY VERSE

Only be careful, and watch yourselves closely so that you do not forget the things your eyes have seen or let them fade from your heart as long as you live. Teach them to your children and to their children after them. (Deuteronomy 4:9, NIV)

QUESTION

Families and churches typically rehearse unique events they experienced to renew their faith in God. Those faith stories demonstrate the activity of God in some memorable way. What unique stories of faith does your family or church regularly rehearse?

INTRODUCTION

Memory—we don't seem to have much use for it these days. Our smartphones remember our phone numbers and appointments for us. Our GPS gives turn-by-turn directions. If we want to know something, we just do a quick online search, or ask our talking smart devices for the answer. There was a time when people had to remember vital information. The culture of people in biblical times relied heavily on oral tradition. People cultivated their memories and passed stories down from generation to generation. Scholars agree that less than ten percent of people during Jesus'

time were literate, so ancient Israel passed down their faith and history through memorizing and retelling their stories. With that in mind, consider how essential memory was for their faith formation.

BLACK HISTORY SPOTLIGHT: Freedmen's Village in Arlington, Virginia

One of the most important aspects of the Civil War and emancipation is the variety of ways African Americans pursued their freedom. African American liberation extended far beyond the Emancipation Proclamation and Juneteenth. Even before either of those proclamations, many slaves simply packed up what they had and abandoned the plantations and farms on which they lived. Throughout the war, military authorities in and around the Washington, D.C., area struggled to find a solution to the overcrowding in the contraband camps. The fact that the area included two states and a district with different laws regarding slavery added complexity.

The American Missionary Association and the Freedmen's Relief Association, two organizations that wanted to help African Americans, worked with the War Department to set up a contraband village outside the capital. Because these organizations viewed the military camps in Washington, D.C., as a humanitarian crisis, they believed that establishing a village outside the crowded capital would make life better for the African American contrabands. At the same time, the organizations believed that a camp away from the capital would make it easier for them to help educate and evangelize African Americans.

All they needed to set up a community was a location, and fortunately a location was already under Union control. In 1861, the Union Army seized the property of General Robert E. Lee and his wife, Martha Custis Lee. Located right across the Potomac River in Arlington, Virginia, it was a perfect location to move the African American contrabands. By the summer of 1863, the military had constructed the village and started transferring them there. In December of that same year, the military sponsored a celebration formally dedicating Freedmen's Village. Many White residents in Arlington County, however, did not approve of the resettlement project. An editorial in the *Arlington Gazette* openly questioned the value of moving the formerly enslaved people to Freedman's village and hoped that "surplus stock [contrabands at Freedmen's Village] were moved in the same direction [they came from]." Nevertheless, within a year, the village consisted of approximately fifty duplex homes that accommodated two families each.[1]

There was much more to Freedmen's Village than just residential homes. Unlike the military camps, the creators of the village wanted it to be more like a community. They constructed a hospital, church, and industrial school. Mount Zion Baptist Church, the first of three Black churches in Freedmen's Village served as the pillar of the community. Mount Zion was the most important and visible institution in the village and it not only attended to the spiritual and educational needs of the community, but it also was the location of numerous town meetings and political conventions.

The government eventually closed Freedmen's Village in 1900, leaving no trace of the community that once thrived there. Nevertheless, the legacy of the community and the people who created and lived in Freedmen's Village remains at Arlington House, the old plantation house. The museum there and the grounds stand not only as a memorial to the war and all the members and persons connected with one of the South's most famous families, but it also stands as a testament to the lives lived, lost, and forgotten by history in Freedmen's Village.

---

[1] "From the Washington Chronicle." *The Arlington Gazette*, July 14, 1864. From the Library of Congress Website Chronicling America: Historic American Newspapers, https://chroniclingamerica.loc.gov/lccn/sn85025007/1864-07-14/ed-1/seq-2. "Local News" *Evening Star*, Dec. 2, 1863

SCRIPTURE REFERENCES

(Joshua 4:1-7)

1 When the whole nation had finished crossing the Jordan, the LORD said to Joshua, "Choose twelve men from among the people, one from each tribe, 3 and tell them to take up twelve stones from the middle of the Jordan, from right where the priests are standing, and carry them over with you and put them down at the place where you stay tonight." 4 So Joshua called together the twelve men he had appointed from the Israelites, one from each tribe, 5 and said to them, "Go over before the ark of the LORD your God into the middle of the Jordan. Each of you is to take up a stone on his shoulder, according to the number of the tribes of the Israelites, 6 to serve as a sign among you. In the future, when your children ask you, 'What do these stones mean?' 7 tell them that the flow of the Jordan was cut off before the ark of the covenant of the LORD. When it crossed the Jordan, the waters of the Jordan were cut off. These stones are to be a memorial to the people of Israel forever".

LESSON FOCUS

In today's passage, stones became memory devices. A child who asked what the stones meant was enough to trigger the memory and story of Israel crossing the Jordan River into the Promised Land. Memory preserved God's sacred act in Israel's hearts and minds. Today's lesson focuses on the value of rehearsing sacred memory for faith formation.

BIBLE BACKGROUND

In Joshua chapter 3, we learn that after 40 years, the twelve tribes of Israel finally entered the Promised Land. Just as God's miraculous acts ushered Moses and Israel out of Egypt, God performed another miracle to escort Joshua and Israel into their new land. The Lord's command to Joshua to cross the Jordan River while it was at flood stage, creating the script for a sacred drama Israel would never forget.

God's presence, symbolized by the Ark of Covenant, preceded the people into the dangerous waters. The Ark contained visible signs and symbols of God's presence. In it were the Law of God and manna. Over it was the mercy seat, a symbol of pardon. These symbols represented God's Word and ordinances.[2]

The Levites, the priestly tribe, carried the Ark into the Jordan. Clearly, this reminded Israel that God desires to take the lead in their lives—even in the most challenging situations. The priests, as persons dedicated to full-time spiritual service, were also depicted as primary leadership figures in Israel. Spiritual leaders were to be liaisons between God and Israel. Seeking God first in the administration of national affairs was priority. We must remember how different Israel's governing practices were from ours. The government in the United States of America is a democracy— that is, the supreme governing power is vested in the people. During Joshua's time, Israel was a theocracy—meaning God was recognized as the supreme civil ruler.

---

[2] Spence-Jones, H. D. M. (Ed.). (1909). *Joshua* (p. 45). London; New York: Funk & Wagnalls Company.

Crossing the Jordan River was a sacred drama that emphasized God as Israel's supreme leader and the Levites as priests bound to focus on God's guidance for the greater good of the nation.

Creating sacred memory was essential for the preservation of Israel's spiritual heritage. One way they did this is through Shema. The term "Shema" means "hear." The Shema is one of two prayers commanded in the Torah. It is to be recited morning and night and Israelites have kept this tradition since ancient times. We see that Judaism recognizes Deuteronomy 6:4-9 as part of the Shema (part two is Deuteronomy 11:13-21; part three is Numbers 15:37-41). The daily repetition of this prayer indicates its fundamental importance in Jewish faith. Elders were to teach the Shema to their children, just like they were to teach children the story connected to the twelve stones in today's passage.

SCRIPTURE EXPLORATION

Joshua selected twelve men, one from each of Israel's tribes, to take stones to build a memorial marking the entrance into the Promised Land. At this time, Israel was a federation of twelve tribes. In a federation, separate entities come together (in this case the twelve tribes) to form a central government. Each of the separate entities retains control of its own internal affairs. By asking for representatives from each of the twelve tribes, the stone-gathering act provided a visual symbol of unity under God.

In children's ministry we often use object lessons to teach a spiritual lesson. An object lesson uses a familiar object as the focus for a lesson; this serves as a practical example of an abstract concept. The object helps make spiritual concepts concrete and easier to understand and to remember. Think of the twelve stones in today's passage as object lessons for Israel. The twelve stones were spiritual catalysts meant to encourage adults to tell the story to their children. Stories are portable containers that transmit values and ethics and faith.

Throughout Israel's history, forgetting God's commandments and decrees caused them to suffer. Remembering what God did for them, said to them, and expected of them was Israel's ongoing challenge. One would think it difficult to forget God's mighty acts. God parted the Red Sea during the exodus, and God parted the Jordan River for Israel to enter the Promised Land. God instructed Israel to remember this dramatic river crossing. The twelve stones memorialized God's deeds and Israel's trust in God's leadership. Think of the faith that the Levites acted on when they entered the Jordan River at flood stage. Remember, the river stopped flowing *after* the Levites stepped into the water (Joshua 3:15-16). The twelve stones became part of Israel's growing list of memorials. The list included feasts and festivals (especially Passover), the Ark of the Covenant, and phylacteries (leather cubes containing Scripture passages for the Shema).

The command to tell the story about the twelve stones highlights the importance of religious education for children. Storytelling involved effective memory devices: visuals, drama (emotion), and participation. We remember what we see, feel, and do. Israel remembered in community. Together they saw the stones, felt the story's passion, and participated in the telling. As they rehearsed the story, they deepened their faith in God, and preserved their spiritual heritage.

CONTEMPORARY COMMUNITY BUILDING: Mother Carr's Farm and Vernon Park Church of God

Today's lesson features memory as a means of discipleship. As an example, take 1 Corinthians 6:9, "Do you not know that your bodies are members of Christ himself?" Internalizing the virtues in this one verse might inspire you to do something to help others improve the physical health of their bodies. Vernon Park Church of God in Lynwood, Illinois, has a ministry focused on encouraging healthy eating by planting, growing, and harvesting foods from the ground that nurture body, mind, and spirit. This ministry is called Mother Carr's Farm, and they make nutritious produce available to people in the area. They also provide information on health, nutrition, and wellness, educating people on how to better take care of their bodies.

DISCUSSION

"WHAT" - THE BASICS

1. Developing sacred memory involves rehearsing experiences that strengthen trust in God. In what ways do you develop sacred memory in your family?

2. In what ways do you develop sacred memory as a gathered community in your church?

3. To what extent does your family or church use memory as a way to develop faith and Christian discipleship?

4. If you were asked to describe the mission of your church, what story would you tell?

"SO WHAT" - DIGGING DEEPER

1. In the eleventh century, before the invention of the printing press, churches were often constructed with large stained glass to tell biblical stories to people who could not read. What ways could churches tell biblical stories to non-readers today?

2. Israel used feasts and festivals to conduct public remembrances of sacred events. Why do you believe it is important to gather in community to remember sacred events?

3. The twelve stones were catalysts to prompt sacred storytelling. What prompts sacred storytelling in your home or congregation?

APPLICATION OF SCRIPTURE

"NOW WHAT?" – ACTION STEPS

Personal

If you wanted to help someone in your family understand God's characteristics or some feature of Christianity, what stories would you tell? Make a list of personal and biblical stories you believe people in your family should know by heart. Make it a point to take turns telling the story from the oldest to the youngest in your household.

Congregational

How might your congregation make public acts of remembrance, like communion or baptism, more memorable? Consider the role of drama, liturgical dance, music, congregational participation, sight, and sound. Consider passages of Scripture that your congregation should learn by heart during public acts of remembrance. Next, identify the Christian virtue embedded in the passage of Scripture and invite people to express that virtue in their daily lives. Consider sharing testimonials of ways people are living their faith in real and tangible ways.

MEDITATION

Repeat to remember. Remember to repeat. Dear Lord, we gather for the Lord's Supper and say, "Do this in remembrance of me." In community, we rehearse the story to keep what You did for us on Calvary's cross on our minds. Help us remember to repeat. There is so much more to recall. You care for us, guide us, comfort and discipline us. You do this because You love us. Help us remember to repeat. When drifting in the sea of hardship, what life-preserving stories will keep us afloat? We embrace our responsibility to remember to repeat faith stories: in our families, while at work, and when we gather for worship.

PRAYER

Gracious God, we often say "If you can see it, you can be it." When the world tries to squeeze us into its mold, show us the pathway to Christ-like behavior. When the media tempts us to buy the latest thing we don't need, show us images of contentment. When we experience heartbreak, show us redeeming stories to heal our souls. Create in us a Christian vision that always sees the righteous way through life. Amen.

BIBLIOGRAPHY

Peer Press. *Brain Rules* by John Medina. www.brainrules.net. http://www.brainrules.net/about-brain-rules Retrieved November 11, 2017.

Rich, Tracy. Judaism 101, *Shema*. www.jewfaq.org. http://www.jewfaq.org/shemaref.htm Retrieved November 11, 2017.

Spence-Jones, H. D. M. (Ed.). (1909). *Joshua* (p. 45). London; New York: Funk & Wagnalls Company.

Steele, D., & Terry, M. S. (1901). *Joshua to II Samuel*. (D. D. Whedon, Ed.) (Vol. III, p. 33). New York; Cincinnati: Eaton & Mains; Jennings & Graham.

Theology of Work Project. (2014–2016). *Genesis through Revelation*. (W. Messenger, Ed.) (Vol. 2, pp. 9–10). Peabody, MA: Hendrickson Publishers.

RECOMMENDED RESOURCES:

Peer Press. *Brain Rules* by John Medina. www.brainrules.net. http://www.brainrules.net/about-brain-rules Retrieved November 11, 2017.

Rich, Tracy. Judaism 101, *Shema*. www.jewfaq.org. http://www.jewfaq.org/shemaref.htm Retrieved November 11, 2017.

Theology of Work Project. (2014–2016). *Genesis through Revelation*. (W. Messenger, Ed.) (Vol. 2). Peabody, MA: Hendrickson Publishers.

Holmes, Barbara Ann. *Joy Unspeakable: Contemplative Practices of the Black Church*. Minneapolis: Augsburg Press, 2004.

NOTES

_____

_____

_____

_____

_____

_____

_____

_____

_____

CHAPTER 9

Rahab Helps to Build

Scripture Lesson: Joshua 2:15-16, 6:1-5
Background Scriptures: Joshua 2, 6

MEMORY VERSE

When the trumpets sounded, the army shouted, and at the sound of the trumpet, when the men gave a loud shout, the wall collapsed; so everyone charged straight in, and they took the city. (Joshua 6:20, NIV)

QUESTION

We regularly encounter moral conflict in our everyday lives. For example, we believe that telling the truth is always morally right. Taking marriage as an example, consider the following situations:

A. A wife asks her husband, "Does this dress make me look fat?"

B. A husband says to his wife, "I should handle our money because I **know** what I'm doing. Isn't that right, babe?"

Depending on the answer, speaking the truth seems to compete with keeping good marital relationships.

Prompt: You are faced with the above moral conflicts—should you tell the truth or keep peace in the relationship? Are telling the truth and keeping peace mutually exclusive? Assuming the *truthful* answers to both of the questions is no, how would you answer? Explain your response.

INTRODUCTION

When plunged into a high-stakes situation, what happens to your moral compass? Does the needle always point true north with clear-cut choices? What happens if telling the truth could hurt someone's feelings? Do you get conflicted? How do you maintain relationship *and* maintain your moral integrity? How does one maintain moral integrity while confronting difficult situations? In today's lesson, we find Rahab in the midst of a moral dilemma. She has to decide between telling the truth about housing Israelite spies, or telling a lie to save their lives, yet put her own life at risk. The passage in today's lesson reveals her choice and the benefit Israel received because of her decision.

BLACK HISTORY SPOTLIGHT: Tuskegee, Alabama

Throughout Macon County in Tuskegee, Alabama, African Americans desperately wanted a school that could train future educators, farmers, and tradesmen. With a predominantly Black population, this town had the opportunity to be a hub for all the rural townships outside Tuskegee, including Macedonia and Notasulga. Most of the residents of these towns in the 1880s were tenants and often moved from farm to farm. But some early leaders did emerge.

Lewis Adams was born a slave in 1842. By 1880, the skilled shoemaker had established himself as a farmer and political boss of Tuskegee's Black community. During that year, two Democratic Party candidates for office approached Adams asking for his support. Adams promised to endorse the candidates with the condition that they support building a normal school for African Americans in Macon County. After their election, the two politicians kept their promise and sponsored a bill in the State House creating the Tuskegee Normal School for training Black teachers. Adams worked closely with George Washington Campbell, an insurance broker and former slave master, to lay the groundwork for what would become Tuskegee Institute. Campbell and Adams contacted Samuel Chapman Armstrong to ask for suggestions for a leader of the new school. Chapman, remembering his old student, nominated Booker T. Washington, who became the school's first principal.[1]

One noticeable thing about the Tuskegee community is how long its reach was. Older residents united with educators and recent migrants to create a community that pushed residents toward financial and social independence. As more Blacks moved to Tuskegee, other businesses and services, in addition to the institute, came to the town including grocers, dentists, physicians, and planters. By 1900, a well-established business community lived near the institute. The community also built the only hospital in the region for African Americans.

Religious life was an important aspect of Tuskegee life. There were a number of churches around Tuskegee, including the Mount Olive Missionary Baptist Church, which was the church that Washington attended. Another important church was the Butler Chapel African Methodist Episcopal Zion Church. Butler Chapel was founded in 1865 by Reverend John M. Butler. It was the initial location of Tuskegee Normal School. It is reported that Solomon Derry, the second pastor of Butler Chapel, was one of the first Black teachers in Macon County and that he had a school with 250 students.[2]

Religious life went beyond church services. Tuskegee Institute had a Bible Training School on campus that regularly worked at developing local ministers. These classes were not just Bible training sessions; they focused on helping local ministers develop a more progressive spirit. Washington encouraged local ministers to link spiritual matters with race progress. At a ministers' institute meeting in 1906, Washington encouraged ministers to "encourage our young men to go into business. The financial hope of our race rests largely on our young men going into business.

---

[1] Amalia K. Amaki and Amelia Boynton Robinson, *Tuskegee* (Alabama: Arcadia Publishing, 2013), 26-7; Washington, *Up From Slavery*, 120.

[2] "History," *Mt. Olive Missionary Baptist Church* (Tuskegee, AL) http://www.mtolivebaptistchurchtuskegee.org/history, assessed December 8, 2017.

The church will be better off financially. ... We must teach our people to spend their money with friends of the race."[3]

Washington's dreams of an independent Black community may not have been completely realized. His final speech in 1915 occurred right before the major urban migrations throughout the South. Blacks would never again own as much land as they did in 1915. However, the institution he built and the Black community that congregated around it remain more than a century after his death. Tuskegee University remains an excellent institution of higher learning that continues to inspire the town and surrounding community. Nevertheless, it is important to remember two things about the success of Tuskegee: (1) Black people prospered because they adopted a plan of self-determination and property ownership, and (2) Black people in Tuskegee were willing to collaborate with people many may not consider likely partners. Just as the Israelites' relationship with Rahab led to their success at Jericho, African Americans' relationship with unlikely partners led to Tuskegee's success.

SCRIPTURE REFERENCES

(Joshua 2:15-16)

15 So she [Rahab] let them down by a rope through the window, for the house she lived in was part of the city wall. 16 She said to them, "Go to the hills so the pursuers will not find you. Hide yourselves

there three days until they return, and then go on your way."

(Joshua 6:1-5)

1 Now the gates of Jericho were securely barred because of the Israelites. No one went out and no one came in. 2 Then the LORD said to Joshua, "See, I have delivered Jericho into your hands, along with its king and its fighting men. 3 March around the city once with all the armed men. Do this for six days. 4 Have seven priests carry trumpets of rams' horns in front of the ark. On the seventh day, march around the city seven times, with the priests blowing the trumpets. 5 When you hear them sound a long blast on the trumpets, have the whole army give a loud shout; then the wall of the city will collapse and the army will go up, everyone straight in."

LESSON FOCUS

Is it okay to break one moral principle to fulfill the requirements of another one? How do you make faithful choices when facing personal danger? The backstory of today's passage helps us understand how important it is to make moral choices through the lens of faith in God. Let us see what Rahab's choice can teach us about discerning God's will when experiencing moral conflict.

BIBLE BACKGROUND

Lying is wrong; ask anyone on the street. All people, religious or not, have some rule in their moral code that detests lying. A quick survey of Scripture reveals consistent denunciation of lying. The ninth

---

[3] *The Messenger*, April 20, 1906,

commandment says "You shall not give false testimony against your neighbor" (Exodus 20:16). While Israel wandered in the wilderness, Moses told them,

"Do not steal. Do not lie. Do not deceive one another" (Leviticus 19:11). Proverbs, part of biblical wisdom literature, declares that God hates "a lying tongue" (Proverbs 6:17). The book of Revelation contains the most sober warning to liars, lumping them in a category along with murderers and those who practice witchcraft. It says, "they will be consigned to the fiery lake of burning sulfur" (Revelation 21:8).

Given these strong prohibitions against lying, it seems strange that Scripture appears to commend Rahab for acting deceitfully. When asked by representatives from the king of Jericho to turn over the spies from Israel, she tells them "At dusk, when it was time to close the city gate, they left. I don't know which way they went . . ." (Joshua 2:5). Disobeying a royal command could have cost Rahab her life.

Rahab's story raises moral questions for us to ponder. Are we free to obey God's law sometimes and ignore it at other times? Is it okay to lie to a bad person, but not okay to lie to a good person? Should we, like Rahab, lie to save ourselves from harm? What lessons are we to learn from Rahab's actions?

A concept from the legal system can help us sort through the moral dilemma posed by Rahab's story. The term *prima facie* (pry-mah fay-shah), which means "at first sight" or "at first glance," describes a court case that seems clear cut **unless** there is substantial contradictory evidence

presented at trial. At first glance, Rahab appears to be lying to save the men who had visited her inn; but there are other factors to consider. In Rahab's case, the contradictory evidence is her faith in Israel's God. The text records Rahab saying this after learning about what God had done through Israel: "When we heard of it, our hearts melted in fear and everyone's courage failed because of you, for the LORD your God is God in heaven above and on the earth below" (Joshua 2:11). Rahab lied because her allegiance to God outranked her allegiance to the king of Jericho. Scripture rehearses Rahab's story because she was willing to put her life at risk to advance God's cause.

According to Matthew 1:5, Rahab became the wife of Salmon and the mother of Boaz—who married Ruth. Family lineage was very important to Jewish people. Thus, it is no small thing that Matthew lists Rahab in Jesus' genealogy. Rahab also makes the "faith hall of fame" in Hebrews. The writer of Hebrews says "By faith the prostitute Rahab, because she welcomed the spies, was not killed with those who were disobedient" (Hebrews 11:31).

SCRIPTURE EXPLORATION

Today's passage reveals the moral choice Rahab made. Based on what she had heard about the Lord and Israel, she chose to lie to save the lives of the Israelite spies. The reports about God's exploits caused her and others in her city to "melt in fear." These powerful acts of God convinced her that Jericho's king and army were no match for God. Others in Jericho may have shared the same sentiment, but Rahab acted on her newfound faith in God. Some scholars believe part of the Israelite spies' mission was to determine whether people in Jericho respected Yahweh. Rahab helped the spies to escape, which aided God's plan for Israel to occupy Jericho.

In Joshua 6, we see Rahab's assertion confirmed that God's power was superior to Jericho's military might. Jericho was an important city. Scholars propose several possible origins for Jericho's name. The proposal most appropriate to our lesson says Jericho may have been associated with the ancient name of the Canaanite moon god. If that is the case, Israel's triumph over Jericho was a triumph over that nation's allegiance to another god—an echo of God's triumph over Pharaoh and Egypt's many gods.

Interestingly, God's instructions for taking the city resembled more of a religious ritual than a military strategy. The pre-battle ceremony included circling Jericho for six days. On the seventh day, seven priests blew their trumpets in front of the Ark as it was carried into a war zone. Trumpets were only used by priests to announce festivals and to give signals of war.[4] This type of strategy was unprecedented in the Ancient Near East. The sign of God's presence (the Ark) and Israel's obedience to God's guidance provided the power necessary to shatter Jericho's walls.

Rahab's faith-inspired moral choice contributed to Israel's victory over the king of Jericho and his army. What moral choice could we make today to bless others in the future?

CONTEMPORARY COMMUNITY BUILDING: Network of Woodlawn

Just as Rahab's moral decision contributed to the future welfare of others, the moral decisions made by community organizations can have far-reaching effects. This can be seen the work of Dr. Byron Brazier III, pastor of the Apostolic Church of God in Chicago, Illinois. He is the board chairman of the Network of Woodlawn. The Network of Woodlawn is a Chicago organization first founded in 1960 to address neighborhood challenges. The organization targeted substandard housing, insufficient job opportunities, and inadequate city services. Today, the Network of Woodlawn partners with other organizations to revitalize the Woodlawn community through better education, job training, and financial assistance. Individually and organizationally, God works through our moral decisions to improve the lives of others.

DISCUSSION

"WHAT" - THE BASICS

1. When facing a moral dilemma, what guides your thought process? Share any critical questions or moral framework that shape your thoughts.

2. We often hear people diminish lying by saying something is a white lie. Would you say Rahab told a white lie? If not, how would you justify her actions?

---

[4] Easton, M. G. (1893). In *Easton's Bible dictionary*. New York: Harper & Brothers.

3. Scripture says, "The gates of Jericho were securely barred because of the Israelites. No one went out and no one came in" (Joshua 6:1). Why do you believe the king of Jericho wanted to bar Israel from entering Jericho's gates?

"SO WHAT" - DIGGING DEEPER

1. What from today's study of Rahab helped you understand the motives behind her decision to help the Israelite spies?

2. Review God's instructions to Israel for the conquest of Jericho in Joshua 6:2–5. What do these unorthodox instructions teach you about God's strategy for overcoming Jericho?

3. God instructed Israel to conduct a ritual ceremony (circling Jericho seven days, carrying the Ark of the Covenant, blowing trumpets by priests, and shouts from the larger community). What do you believe happened to the people *while* they were participating in these moments? How has your participation in sacred rituals helped you or others through difficult situations? Share concrete examples.

APPLICATION OF SCRIPTURE

"NOW WHAT?" – ACTION STEPS

Personal

Think about a moral dilemma you have experienced in the past. With today's discussion in mind, what would you do differently if you had another chance to respond? Write your response down or discuss your response with another person. In what ways would your revised response glorify God and uphold God's moral standards?

Congregational

Invite your pastor and other leaders to address the importance of making moral decisions in everyday life. Options may include the following: 1. a short-term study using a book such as *Crucial Conversations: Tools for Talking When Stakes are High*. 2. a sermon series highlighting moral dilemmas using biblical characters like Samson and Jezebel; David and Bathsheba; Ananias and Sapphira; Paul and Peter (Circumcision and new Gentile Christian converts); Sadducees and the Roman government (political influence over religion). Find parallel contemporary examples for each sermon. The ultimate aim of such explorations is to underscore the importance of building one's life, ministry, or organization on firm moral footing.

MEDITATION

How often do we feel "in between?" Between a rock and a hard place when our jobs ask us to ignore protocol—"just this time." Between a rock and a hard place when your family members ask you to "do a little something" to keep them out of trouble. Between a rock and a hard place when a situation tempts you to cross a line "for a good cause." When a "rock and hard place" pressure us, Lord, lead us to moral high ground.

PRAYER

Lord, Your ways are far above our ways. Your view from above sees the big picture when shortsightedness obscures our vision. Your view spans the beginning and end of time, while ours only sees the momentary predicament we're in. When the right thing and the wrong motive tug us east and west, point our moral compass north to Your perfect will. Amen.

BIBLIOGRAPHY

Easton, M. G. In *Easton's Bible Dictionary*. New York: Harper & Brothers, 1893.

Elwell, W. A., & Beitzel, B. J. Jericho. In *Baker Encyclopedia of the Bible* (Vol. 2, p. 1118). Grand Rapids, MI: Baker Book House, 1988.

Patterson, Kerry, Joseph Grenny, Ron McMillan, Al Switzler. *Crucial Conversations: Tools for Talking When Stakes are High*. New York: McGraw Hill, 2012.

Schuurman, Douglas J. *Vocation: Discerning our Callings in Life*. Grand Rapids: Eerdmans, 2004.

RECOMMENDED RESOURCES:

Patterson, Kerry, Joseph Grenny, Ron McMillan, Al Switzler. *Crucial Conversations: Tools for Talking When Stakes are High*. New York: McGraw Hill, 2012.

NOTES

_____

_____

_____

_____

_____

_____

CHAPTER 10

Building Tomorrow Today

Scripture Lesson: Joshua 24:13-15
Background Scriptures: Joshua 24:1-28

MEMORY VERSE

This stone will be a witness against us. It has heard all the words the LORD has said to us. It will be a witness against you if you are untrue to your God. (Joshua 24:27, NIV)

QUESTION

Many of us have heard the Edmund Burke quote "Those who don't know history are destined to repeat it." Think about your family's history. Which experiences (good and bad) have taught you the most important life lessons? Share an example.

INTRODUCTION

Celebrating church anniversaries is a regular fixture in Black church culture. We celebrate to remember the road we trod. We celebrate to honor the birth of our church. We recall who founded it and the sacrifices made to build it. We celebrate to rehearse the sacred memory of the journey our church made: the setbacks we overcame and the victories experienced. We celebrate to honor the God who called us to be a unique congregation dedicated to love God, love neighbor, and "treat everybody right." Young people need to hear the social and political functions the church and its leaders served "back in the day." Seasoned saints need to

be reminded that they are part of a lasting legacy. Telling the story remains a celebrated practice that must continue— provided the story arms us with helpful knowledge from the past that informs how we will walk with God into the future.

BLACK HISTORY SPOTLIGHT:
Freedmen's Town, Houston, Texas

Juneteenth, the day Texas freed its slaves, had tremendous ramifications for Houston, Texas. Between 1850 and 1860, slaves made up more than 20 percent of the city's population. Many of them, almost all formerly enslaved people, lived in the area directly adjoining the city's downtown area known as the Fourth Ward. In 1841, the Methodist church organized a church there. Included in the approximately 70 founding members were 32 African Americans. Ten years later, Black people had formed their own church, with a white minister as required by law. This church seems to have been very forward thinking for the period in that it was not simply interested in attending to the believers' spiritual needs, but it also was involved in promoting social issues. In 1858, a local newspaper reported that there was a school in the African Methodist Episcopal Church.[1]

Waves of African American freed persons migrated to Houston and, in particular, the Fourth Ward. Invigorated by their newfound freedom, formerly enslaved men and women moved from the rural plantations into urban environments in search of jobs and a new life. Many of these freed people came from the vast cotton plantations along the Brazos River, taking San Felipe Road directly to the Fourth Ward. Eventually, Black people would refer to this area as Freedmen's Town. The population of the area grew considerably because of the migration. Between 1870 and 1910, the Black population rose from approximately 1,300 to 6,400.[2]

Though the Black community in Fourth Ward was not as financially as well off as those in Jackson Ward in Richmond, Virginia or Greenwood in Tulsa, Oklahoma, the community did demonstrate a remarkable dedication to looking forward. In addition to having a number of masonic lodges and other similar organizations, local leaders focused their activism toward building schools and institutions that would enhance the future of the next generation. By the early twentieth century, the community had a variety of businesses, restaurants, a movie theater, and a park where Negro league baseball teams played.[3]

These transitions in Fourth Ward led to it emerging as Houston's main hub of African American activity. After 1870, as the Fourth Ward became much more segregated, a process that would continue until the 1920s, Black people started moving to the Third and Fifth wards, which had more room to expand. Nevertheless, the largest years of growth in the Fourth Ward, from 1870 to 1920, demonstrate a community that looked very much to the future.

As the district became better established, more Black professionals moved into the area. One of the most important things that happened to the community was the development of the Ancient Order of Pilgrims, a fraternal organization established in 1882 for the specific purpose of helping Blacks. This organization, like similar ones, provided insurance and loans to its members. In 1926, the organization built a beautiful building in the Fourth Ward. This building not only housed the organization, but it also provided rental spaces for other Black-owned businesses. This was where the Black chamber of commerce met, led in the early years by H. Spivey and O.K. Manning, one of the chamber's first secretaries. N.A. Franklin also had her beauty school in the building.[4]

[1] Cary D. Wintz, "The Emergence of a Black Neighborhood: Houston's Fourth Ward, 1865-1915 in *Urban Texas: Politics and Development* ed. by Char Miller and Heywood T. Sanders, 96-100.

[2] Wintz, 99-100

[3] Jarred Stewart, "Buffalo Stadium and Segregated Baseball," *East Texas History*, accessed December 10, 2017, http://easttexashistory.org/items/show/163; Rob Fink, *Playing in Shadows: Texas and Negro League Baseball* (Lubbock, TX: Texas Tech University Press, 2010)

[4] Priscilla Graham, *Texas Historical African American Historical Markers* (Lulu: 2016), 78.

In 1910, Black doctors organized in the Fourth Ward and established the Union Hospital. This hospital was the only African Americans hospital in Houston until the Houston Negro Hospital opened in 1923. By the 1920s, however, residents of the Fourth Ward realized that even though their community had tremendous history, its location and residential segregation, meant that there was little room for their community to grow. Because of its location in an expanding downtown location, the Second Ward did not have suburban property that could be purchased and subdivided for African Americans. The Third Ward (and later the Fifth Ward), by contrast, had more area to expand. By the 1920s, the Third Ward surpassed the Fourth Ward in population. A new high school for African Americans, the second in the city, was erected in the 1920s, as well as a hospital. Houston Negro Junior College, which would later become Texas Southern University, was moved to the Third Ward, a choice that would ensure that the Third Ward would become the center of Black-owned businesses and social community. The final breaking point for the Fourth Ward happened during World War II when, by the use of eminent domain, the city acquired 38 acres of property in the ward to create San Felipe Courts, a housing project restricted to White military families. Even though the Black land owners fought the acquisition in the Supreme Court, their petition was rejected. Worse yet, the city erected a wall between San Felipe Courts and the Black community. Other damage was down to the community, including the destruction of the Black branch of Carnegie Library to make for the interstate expansion. The library had been constructed by William Pittman, son-in-law of Booker T. Washington.[5]

Even though very little remains of old Freedmen's Town today, its legacy remains in the bricks made to pave the streets. In the early twentieth century, without assistance from the city, local African Americans paved the streets with the bricks they made. It is possible that some of those bricks were laid by formerly enslave people. These bricks survive today, standing as a testament that African Americans have always believed in building tomorrow today.

SCRIPTURE REFERENCES

(Joshua 24:13-15, NIV)

13 So I gave you a land on which you did not toil and cities you did not build; and you live in them and eat from vineyards and olive groves that you did not plant.' 14 "Now fear the LORD and serve him with all faithfulness. Throw away the gods your ancestors worshiped beyond the Euphrates River and in Egypt, and serve the LORD. 15 But if serving the LORD seems undesirable to you, then choose for yourselves this day whom you will serve, whether the gods your ancestors served beyond the Euphrates, or the gods of the Amorites, in whose land you are living. But as for me and my household, we will serve the LORD."

---

[5] Wintz, 106; Steven Strom, *Houston Lost and Unbuilt* (Austin: University of Texas Press, 2010), 23; Claudia Feldman, "Is it too late to save Freedmen's Town?" *Houston Chronicle*, http://www.houston-chronicle.com/news/houston-texas/houston/article/Freedmen-s-Town-dead-or-alive-6829518.php

LESSON FOCUS

San (return). *Ko* (go). *Fa* (look, seek, and take). *Sankofa*, the word from the Akan people in Ghana, literally means, "It is not taboo to fetch what is at risk of being left behind."[6] The saying reminds us that we should examine history carefully and patiently to learn its rich lessons. It also encourages us to gather the best of what the past teaches and use that to enable us to achieve our full potential. Whatever was lost or forsaken can be retrieved and revived.

In today's lesson, Joshua invites the tribes of Israel to experience a "sankofa moment." Israel has finally made it into the Promised Land. Joshua is about to die and calls the twelve-tribe federation together to rehearse its history. This is their chance to declare their spiritual allegiance. They must choose whether they will serve the God who brought them there. This sankofa moment captures their attention through Joshua's riveting storytelling, stern challenges, and dramatic ending— memorialized by a stone witness. Upon this sankofa moment Israel will build its future.

BIBLE BACKGROUND

Joshua summoned the twelve tribes of Israel to Shechem, a place rich in history. At Shechem, God promised Abram the land of Canaan. After a 20-year sojourn in northern Mesopotamia, Jacob returned to Shechem and bought land. After the defilement of their sister Dinah,

Simeon and Levi massacred Shechem's male population in revenge. Shechem later became a refuge city.[7] In the New Testament, some scholars believe Sychar (a possible variant spelling of Shechem), mentioned in John 4, was the place where Jesus encountered the Samaritan woman at the well. Joshua's farewell speech takes place in a location that had its own story to tell.

People in ancient biblical times were steeped in a culture of oral tradition. In those days, history lived as long as communities rehearsed it. The people shared ownership of their story. Joshua possibly learned from his predecessor, Moses, that the people needed periodic reminders of who they were and whose they were. Joshua chose this occasion to remind Israel of her sacred history.

At the beginning of chapter 24, Joshua reminded Israel of the beginning of its sacred journey. God called Abraham from the land beyond the Euphrates River where people served other gods. God brought Abraham to Canaan where his descendants multiplied.

Joshua then rehearsed deliverance stories. God delivered Israel from Egypt, from the Amorites, and from the various inhabitants surrounding Israel's Promised Land.

The deliverance stories reminded Israel of God's favor toward them. Israel occupied land on which they had never labored and enjoyed the fruit of vineyards and olive yards they had never planted. With the

---

[6] University of Illinois Springfield. "Sankofa." www.uis.edu. https://www.uis.edu/africanamericanstudies/students/sankofa/ Retrieved December 10, 2017.

[7] Elwell, W. A., & Beitzel, B. J. (1988). Shechem (Place). In *Baker encyclopedia of the Bible* (Vol. 2, p. 1942). Grand Rapids, MI: Baker Book House.

rehearsal complete, the scene was set for Joshua to issue a "put up or shut up" challenge to Israel.

SCRIPTURE EXPLORATION

Joshua's rehearsal of Israel's sacred story painted a picture of God's providence. God delivered them repeatedly from the hands of their enemies. The Israelites now lived in an established town they did not build, and ate food they did not plant. Joshua's dramatic storytelling led to this climatic question. Will you, Israel, faithfully follow the God that delivered you?

Joshua's demand for the people to throw away the gods their ancestors worshiped and fully serve the LORD indicates the erratic nature of Israel's faith. Israel regularly fell prey to the temptation to serve other gods. Abraham's folks worshiped them beyond the Euphrates. Egypt's many gods enticed them. The gods of the Amorites and other nearby peoples seduced them. The lure of other gods was Israel's Achilles' heel. The first of the Ten Commandments given to Moses states, "I am the LORD your God, who brought you out of Egypt . . . . You shall have no other gods before me" (Exodus 20:2-3).

Joshua then issued a demand: revere the Lord and serve God with all faithfulness. The rich meaning of verse 14 in Hebrew communicates the idea of relating to God blamelessly, with integrity, even in "perfection."[8] To demonstrate their allegiance, Joshua demanded the people to "throw away the gods your ancestors

worshiped beyond the Euphrates River and in Egypt, and serve the LORD." (Joshua 24:14b) No empty-headed nods and vain lip service were sufficient pledges for God. Joshua demanded tangible evidence.

Like a shrewd negotiator, Joshua pressed Israel to declare who they would serve. This was no forced choice, however. If serving God was unacceptable to the people, then they were free to choose the gods Abraham's ancestors worshiped or the gods of the nearby Amorites. Yet, before Israel responded, Joshua revealed where he placed his trust: "But as for me and my household, we will serve the LORD" (Joshua 24:15).

The drama continues beyond today's reading. Israel responded to Joshua by pledging their allegiance to God. Joshua challenged their quick claim: "You are not able to serve the LORD. He is a holy God; he is a jealous God . . ." (Joshua 24:19). Joshua warns them that God will not tolerate their rebellion. The people repeated their claim; more vigorously this time. "No! We will serve the LORD" (Joshua 24:21). With great drama, Joshua names the witnesses to Israel's faith declaration; first, the people themselves, and second, a large stone. "This stone will be a witness against us. It has heard all the words the LORD has said to us. It will be a witness against you if you are untrue to your God" (Joshua 24:27b).

This ends the dramatic event. The rehearsal of sacred history reminded Israel of her sacred journey with God. The people's dramatic declaration to serve God became the spiritual milestone upon which Israel's future would now be built.

---

[8] Howard, D. M., Jr. (1998). *Joshua* (Vol. 5, p. 435). Nashville: Broadman & Holman Publishers.

COMMUNITY DEVELOPMENT BUILDING:
John and Vera Mae Perkins Foundation

John Perkins is a speaker and teacher dedicated to a holistic vision of community. The John and Vera Mae Perkins Foundation is an organization dedicated to racial reconciliation and community development. Through its youth arm, the organization offers after-school tutoring, a summer arts camp, a junior and college internship program, the Good News Bible Club, Young Life Club, and the Jubilee Youth Garden. The foundation also has a housing arm, Zechariah 8, providing affordable housing for low-to-moderate-income families with a focus on single mothers.

DISCUSSION

"WHAT" - THE BASICS

1. What about Joshua's covenant renewal speech do you believe most convinced Israel to renew her allegiance to God?

2. Joshua's rehearsal of Israel's sacred history consisted of both positive memories (God's miraculous interventions) and negative memories (Israel's recurring worship of other gods). Which types of memories have most influenced you to examine your walk with God—the positive ones or the negative ones? Explain.

3. Joshua challenged Israel to throw away the gods their ancestors worshiped. Why do you believe Joshua thought he could challenge Israel's spiritual integrity? Who would you allow to challenge your spiritual integrity? What are the implications of your response?

"SO WHAT" - DIGGING DEEPER

1. Joshua urged Israel to revere the Lord, which means to walk with Him blamelessly, with integrity, and even with "perfection." Using concrete examples, explain what it means to revere the Lord.

2. Joshua rehearsed Israel's history (the good and the bad) to help Israel take an honest look at how it had related to God over the years. What motivates you to take honest inventory of your walk with God? Share examples.

3. Why do you believe Joshua was able to convince Israel to renew its covenant with God? Think about what Joshua shared with Israel and how he communicated his message. What did you learn from his method of persuasion?

APPLICATION OF SCRIPTURE

"NOW WHAT?" – ACTION STEPS

Personal

Create a personal *sankofa* experience. Reminisce about your family history with your parents, grandparents, children, or other family members. Identify the milestone events that most shaped the character of your family members. Explore questions like the following ones:

Did your family resettle during the Great Migration (1915-1960)?

Did any of your family live in or help settle any of the historic Black towns featured in this Vacation Bible School series?

What hardships did your ancestors have to overcome?

To what extent did faith in God influence your family's resolve during hard times?

As you ask questions like these, the story of your family's history should begin taking shape. After identifying important milestones, talk about their significance with your family members. Share the important lessons learned. Make a list of the best memories from your family's past. Reclaim the good things that might have been lost or forsaken. Pledge to build on the lessons learned and reaffirm your trust in God's ability to lead you to a more hopeful future. Write the pledge out on paper, sign it, date it, and keep it in a prominent place as a reminder of your *sankofa* experience and your pledge.

Congregational

Design a "*Sankofa* Sunday" worship experience. Suggestions are:

- Gather important milestone events from your church's archives.

- Interview older saints and longstanding members who remember important parts of your congregation's history.

- Consider making a video collage of the testimonies of those interviewed. The video collage could be played on a loop in the sanctuary as people gather that Sunday.

- Create a visual timeline that highlights the important milestones in your congregation's history. For example, find images, bulletins, or newspaper clippings of the following people and events: 1. The founders; 2. Groundbreaking dates of major church building projects; 3. Spiritual milestones—i.e. strong evangelistic years, important missional/outreach experiences; 4. Community engagement—times when the congregation sponsored or partnered with other entities to help the local community. Place the milestone events on posters and hang them in a prominent place, or create a video or slide presentation of the milestones for inclusion in the worship experience.

- Invite the pastor or a guest speaker to preach a sermon based on Joshua 24.

- Create a responsive reading that rehearses the congregation's sacred journey.

- Create a pledge the congregation could recite in unison to reaffirm the congregant's intent to serve God faithfully in the future.

This would be an ideal time to launch or revise a ministry effort that epitomizes the future direction of the church.

CLOSING WORSHIP

Preparation:

Compile a sample mix of recorded worship music spanning as many decades of the life of your congregation as possible. Play this mix as background music leading up to the closing worship.

On butcher paper, draw the outline of 10 various-sized hands with a wide marker. Write the titles of the lessons you studied together below the hands.

1. Build on Jesus
2. Building a Nation
3. Building Strong Families
4. Skills to Build
5. Building God's House
6. Moses Builds Leaders
7. Building Within Boundaries
8. Joshua's Building Blocks
9. Rahab Helps to Build
10. Building Tomorrow Today

Place the butcher paper on a cloth-covered table. Place a cross in the middle of the table.

While the music is playing, participants should think about the sessions that were most meaningful. Participants may bring an index card they wrote during the week and place it under the session title for which it was written. While at the table, participants may place one of their hands on the hand drawn on the butcher paper

and offer a prayer of thanksgiving for what they learned.

After sharing from the index card(s), the instructor will lead the group through the following responsive reading:

One: We've come this far by faith.

Many: Leaning on the Lord.

One: We've come to remember our journey.

Many: We remember.

One: Why have we come?

Many: To learn how to build lives and communities from the Master.

One: Through whom did the Lord teach us?

Many: Through Abraham and Moses, Rahab and Joshua.

One: What did we learn?

Many: How to build?

One: Build what?

Many: Spiritual Strategies.

One: To do what?

Many: Build God's Church.

One: And build strong families.

Many: And build strong leaders

One: Today we come to remember and rejoice about all we have learned.

Many: Thank God for each lesson learned.

One: But that's not enough! We must do more!

Many: What?

One: We must renew our trust in the Lord.

Many: We do!

One: We must turn from the gods of distraction.

Many: We will!

One: We must offer our gifts in worshipful work.

Many: We shall. We will worship the Lord in all we do.

One: So be it. Amen!

Many: Amen!

UNISON PRAYER

Gracious God, we dare not labor in vain. Our work must help others. There are too many who suffer in need of a kind word, a helping hand, or a compassionate act. Our ancestors struggled to make our lives a little bit better. Help us to labor to create a better future for our children's children. Let us never grow weary in well doing. Remind us that our actions at work and at home bear witness to the Christian faith we claim. May we, like Joshua, say, "as for me and my house, we will serve the Lord." We are our witnesses. You are our witness. We pledge to put to practice what we have learned. Amen.

BIBLIOGRAPHY

Elwell, W. A., & Beitzel, B. J. Shechem (Place). In *Baker Encyclopedia of the Bible* (Vol. 2, p. 1942). Grand Rapids, MI: Baker Book House, 1988.

Howard, D. M., Jr. *Joshua* (Vol. 5, p. 435). Nashville: Broadman & Holman Publishers, 1988.

University of Illinois Springfield. "Sankofa." www.uis.edu. https://www.uis.edu/africanamericanstudies/students/sankofa/ Retrieved December 10, 2017.

NOTES

_____

_____

_____

_____

_____

_____

Answer Key

CHAPTER 1

DISCUSSION

"WHAT" - THE BASICS

1. Read Matthew 7:21-23. What explicit behavior does Jesus warn against? **Jesus warns against claiming to be a disciple, but failing to do the will of God. This even includes people who do things "in the name of the Lord" such as casting out demons and prophesying.**

2. How do you believe this warning relates to the parable of the wise and foolish builders? **The parable highlights the importance of hearing and heeding Jesus' words. We must demonstrate our faith through actions; not just words.**

3. What point is Jesus making in this parable? **We must hear the Lord's words and act on them. Failure to do so leads to foolish decisions that create dire circumstances.**

"SO WHAT" - DIGGING DEEPER

1. Taken together, what are the warning and the parable in Matthew 7 saying to you about being a disciple of Jesus Christ? **Answers will vary.**

2. What has following Christ cost you? **Answers will vary.**

3. After examining today's passage, what do you believe God is asking you to do, be, or change? **Answers will vary.**

CHAPTER 2

DISCUSSION

"WHAT" - THE BASICS

1. What from today's lesson was most challenging to you? **Answers will vary.**

2. The Lord told Abram to leave his country, his people, and his father's household. How challenging would it be for you to do this? Provide specific examples. **Answers will vary.**

3. Think about the attachments that you have established: friends, family, comfort with the familiar, etc. What would it take to convince you to accept God's invitation to leave these close relationships and go to an unfamiliar place? **Answers will vary.**

4. What type of response do you think your family and friends would have if you told them you were leaving your hometown and your country to go where God was leading you? **Answers will vary.**

"SO WHAT" - DIGGING DEEPER

1. What type of spiritual maturity would it take for you to do what Abram did? Describe what would prepare you to

trust God in this situation. **Answers will vary.**

2. Abram had to leave his father's household behind to follow God. When family desires conflict with God's principles, how do you handle those situations? Provide examples. **Answers will vary.**

3. The covenant God initiated with Abram would eventually bless nations. In what ways do you believe your allegiance to Jesus Christ can bless others? **Answers will vary. Possible responses include the following: Serving as a Christian role model who inspires others to exhibit Christian integrity. Being a trusted person that garners favor with organizations willing to help others due to your reputation.**

4. In today's passage, God said to Abram "I will bless those who bless you . . . and all peoples on earth will be blessed through you." What about Abram do you believe would influence God to make such a promise? **Answers will vary. Possible responses include the following: Abram had learned to honor and keep God's covenant. Abram had developed unwavering faith in God. Abram had learned to trust God despite contradicting factors such as Sarai being past normal child-bearing age.**

CHAPTER 3

DISCUSSION

"WHAT" - THE BASICS

1. What does being in covenant with God mean to you? **Answers will vary. The following are typical responses: walking in faithful relationship with God, faithfully keeping the terms of the covenant, ordering my life according to covenant, and allowing covenant to define my life.**

2. Why is the Abrahamic Covenant so significant? **It reveals God's desire to create a people.** What does it establish? **It establishes covenant with Abraham's descendants who become the nation of Israel.**

3. God changed Abram's name to Abraham. How do you believe you would be affected by a name change? **Answers will vary. Examples may include the following: provides a new identity, marks a new beginning, etc.** How would you perceive yourself differently? **Answers will vary.**

"SO WHAT" - DIGGING DEEPER

1. Abram's faith was tested during the 25-year span between Genesis 12 and 17. What are some tests you have had that spurred further spiritual growth and maturity in you? **Answers will vary.**

2. The Abrahamic Covenant was conditional. Abraham had an active role to play to reap its benefits. Beyond saying "Yes, Lord," what conditions do

you believe Christians must satisfy to be in covenant relationship with Jesus Christ? **Answers will vary. Examples may include the following: faithful allegiance to the Lord, love God and neighbor, demonstrate Christianity through word and deed, participate in building the kingdom of God.**

3. Abraham's blood relatives, slaves, and foreigners brought into his household were bound by the Abrahamic Covenant. In what ways are your relatives and members of your household bound by your covenant relationship with Jesus Christ? Explain. **Answers will vary. Examples may include the following: family members must abide by your Christian values when living in your home, family members must respect the call to Christian discipleship on your life.**

4. Through Abraham's covenant relationship with God we learn that the actions of one affect the lives of many. How do you believe the actions of your church affect the quality of life of others in your family and community? Share examples. **Answers will vary. Examples may include the following: learning to be disciples in word and deed influences how members "love their neighbors," churches can create non-profit organizations to provide career training, financial guidance, legal services, housing assistance, etc.**

CHAPTER 4

DISCUSSION

"WHAT" - THE BASICS

1. In what ways did Israel's participation in Passover activities prepare them for their exodus from Egypt? **First, Passover reset Israel's calendar— this indicated a new beginning for them. Second, it promoted unity and sharing—every household participated in this corporate sacrifice. Similarly, households too small to eat a whole lamb had to share with their nearest neighbor. Third, the chosen lambs had to be without defect—they were to give their best offering to God. Fourth, painting the doorposts with lambs' blood instilled faith—doing such an act seemed to be an impractical way to ward off death. Fifth, they learned readiness—they had to eat hurriedly with their cloaks tucked in and sandals on. Last, the day was to be commemorated annua—this e**

2. **mphasized the importance of this event. Participants may discover additional answers.** What divine message did the ten plagues communicate to Pharaoh and Egypt? **Egypt believed in multiple gods; many of them were animals or had animal features. The ten plagues demonstrated God's superiority over Pharaoh and Egypt's gods. From the water supply, to their cherished livestock, to their crops, each plague proved God superior. The final**

plagues targeted the Egyptians and the darkness mocked Pharaoh who considered himself to be the sun god. Finally, the death of Egypt's firstborn completely devastated Pharaoh and the Egyptian religious system. Clearly, God was superior to Pharaoh and Egypt's many gods.

3. What message did the tenth plague send to Israel? **For Israel, God *passing over* them proved God's grace and mercy toward Israel and God's judgment on evil. Participants may share additional answers.**

"SO WHAT" - DIGGING DEEPER

1. Israel had lived in Egypt for hundreds of years. Which harmful habits or attitudes might they have adopted during slavery? **Answers may vary. Examples include the following: a scarcity mentality, acceptance of exploitation from others as normal, pessimism, hopelessness, urge to control, an insatiable appetite for acquiring things, the mindset of an oppressor, etc.**

2. What harmful habits do you believe African Americans developed during slavery that continue to plague our community today? **Answers may vary. Participants may repeat answers from number 1 above. Other examples include the following: color consciousness, distrust of one's racial/ethnic group, uncritical acceptance of double standards, inferiority complex, etc.**

3. Identify a "wilderness" facing you today. What would "worshiping in the wilderness" look like in your situation? **Answers will vary.**

4. Which gifts, abilities, and talents do you believe you could use in your wilderness? **Answers will vary.**

CHAPTER 5

DISCUSSION

"WHAT" - THE BASICS

1. Were you ever asked to make a donation that caused your head (logic) to argue with you heart (compassion)? What did the argument sound like? **Answers will vary.**

2. Why do you believe God asked for offerings from people whose heart prompted them to give? What purpose would that serve? **Possible responses include the following: God loves a cheerful giver. God prefers willing obedience. (Note: God honored Adam and Eve's freewill choices in the Garden of Eden) The Israelites needed to learn to give to God in response to God's goodness evidenced through Israel's divine deliverance from Egypt and providential care in the wilderness.**

3. The Tabernacle was a visual reminder of God's presence. What reminds you of God's presence daily? How does that reminder influence your actions? **Answers will vary.**

4. How was carrying out God's precise instructions for building the sanctuary a spiritual exercise? **Following God's exact instructions demonstrated strict obedience to God's commands.**

"SO WHAT" - DIGGING DEEPER

1. Why do you believe God asked Israel to give precious items to build the sanctuary? **Possible answers include the following: The Hebrews had to determine what they valued most, the precious items or their love for God. Giving the precious items demonstrated allegiance and faith. (Note: Israel later used gold to fashion a golden calf as an idol. See Exodus 32:2-4.)**

2. God had spoken through Moses to deliver Israel from Egypt and to care for them in the wilderness. Why do you believe God now instructed Israel to build God a sanctuary? **Israel needed a daily reminder of God's presence. For generations, Israel witnessed Egypt's religion featuring many gods. In the wilderness, they encountered people who worshiped other gods. The Hebrews must have been tempted to follow suit because the first of the Ten Commandments Moses had shared with them says, "I am the LORD your God, who brought you out of Egypt, out of the land of slavery. You shall have no other gods before me." (Exodus 20:2-3)**

3. In what ways do you believe seeing the Tabernacle daily influenced Israel? **The Tabernacle reminded them of God's overwhelming presence. The Holy of Holies reminded them of God's sacred nature. The Holy Place reminded them to worship God. In short, the Tabernacle was a constant visual reminder that God dwelled among them; a point that should have influenced the choices they made daily.**

CHAPTER 6

DISCUSSION

"WHAT" - THE BASICS

1. What do you believe motivated Jethro to offer leadership advice to Moses? **Answers will vary. Possible responses include the following: As a father-in-law, Jethro cared for Moses' wellbeing and offered advice to ease Moses' burden. Jethro had compassion on the people suffering in line waiting too long to get their concerns heard.**

2. Why do you believe Moses tried to shoulder so much leadership responsibility? **Answers will vary. Possible responses include the following: Moses might have felt that the primary burden of leadership rested on him because God called him to lead Israel. God allowed Aaron to share in leadership as a concession to Moses who was insecure initially. (See Exodus 4:10-16)** What can you learn about leadership from your conclusions? **Answers will vary.**

3. What leadership lessons can we learn from Jethro's example? **Answers will vary. Possible responses include the following: Good leaders care about others and offer compassion-based advice. Wise leaders know how to develop orderly systems. Good leadership requires people of good character. Wise leaders develop people with good character and spiritual maturity who can become leaders.**

"SO WHAT" - DIGGING DEEPER

1. What were the major action steps in Jethro's recommendations to Moses? **(1) He assessed the status quo: He pointed out how the flaws in current practice were harming Moses and the people. (2) He reviewed the job description: Moses main job was to be God's representative. (3) He recommended spiritual instruction: Moses needed to teach God's decrees and instructions. (4) He advised intentional character development: Moses needed to demonstrate how the people should live and behave. (5) He provided leadership qualifications: Leaders should be people of good character. (6) He suggested delegating power and authority: The new leaders were to serve as judges over smaller cases. (7) He suggested an orderly process: The officials were over people in a hierarchy—tens, fifties, hundreds, and thousands.** Which of Jethro's recommendations does your local church use to develop leaders? **Answers will vary.**

2. Which character traits did Jethro state potential leaders needed to demonstrate? **God-fearing, trustworthy, unwilling to solicit dishonest gain.** Think of a specific leadership position in your local church. Which character traits would a person need to demonstrate to be considered for leadership for that position? **Answers will vary.**

3. In today's passage, people waited in line from morning until evening to get a hearing about their concerns. In addition to waiting for justice, what do you believe people can or should do to address their concerns? **Answers will vary. Possible responses include the following: The people can proactively participate in developing solutions to their problems. People can seek advocates to plead their case in higher places.**

CHAPTER 7

DISCUSSION

"WHAT" - THE BASICS

1. In what ways does Israel's wilderness story mirror the post-slavery story of African Americans? Name some of the similar challenges faced by the newly freed Israelites and the newly freed African Americans. **Both groups suffered forced enslavement. Both groups had to contend with the psychological effects of enslavement after they were freed. Both groups depended on God's guidance and care to build viable communities.**

2. Why do you believe Israel needed to heed God's decrees in preparation for establishing a permanent community in the Promised Land? **Answers may vary. Sample responses include the following: At Baal Peor, the Israelites tried to live apart from God's commands and guidance and reaped punishment from God. (Deuteronomy 4:3) Neighboring nations would view Israel as a nation of wise and understanding people—this reputation would likely help Israel's international relations.**

3. In what ways do you believe obeying God's decrees (like the Ten Commandments) distinguished Israel from neighboring nations? Give examples. **Answers may vary. Sample responses include the following: In the Promised Land, Israel would be settling in an area with nations whose communities were not based on God's laws and decrees. Israel needed to obey God's decrees to prevent its members from reverting to the oppressive behaviors witnessed in Egypt or witnessed in other nations. Obeying God's decrees would help Israel become a wise, understanding people.**

"SO WHAT" - DIGGING DEEPER

1. In what ways did Israel's memory of Pharaoh and Egyptian oppression continue to cause Israel problems? **They could not imagine a future outside the oppressive existence they had in Egypt. They reminisced about their time in Egypt as if those were** the "good old days" (Exodus 16:3 and Numbers 11:5).

2. Read Exodus 20:1-6. Why do you believe God needed to spend time reminding Israel about their deliverance by God's hand? **Israel needed to reaffirm their faith in the God who delivered them from Pharaoh and Egypt's oppressive rule. Their divine deliverance from bondage in Egypt should have established God's supremacy in their hearts and minds. The fact that Israel murmured in the wilderness and tried to live apart from God's commands in Baal Peor indicate its spiritual amnesia.** What has God done for you that you need to remember and reaffirm your faith? **Answers will vary.**

3. In what ways do you believe remembering God's words and deeds helped strengthen community in Israel? Share specific examples. **Answers will vary. Sample responses include the following: Remembering God's acts strengthened Israel's faith in God as Deliverer and Provider. Remembering was an act of worship that kept God centered in the community's mind.**

4. How does remembering God's words and deeds strengthen your church community? Share specific examples. **Answers will vary.**

CHAPTER 8

DISCUSSION

"WHAT" - THE BASICS

1. Developing sacred memory involves rehearsing experiences that strengthen trust in God. In what ways do you develop sacred memory in your family? **Answers will vary. Possible responses include the following: Ritual practices—like blessing meals, nightly prayers, and daily devotions. Storytelling—repeating family faith stories until each family member can retell them, performing charitable acts and explaining them as normal Christian responses. The repeated practice of charitable acts makes them normative behaviors.**

2. In what ways do you develop sacred memory as a gathered community in your church? **Answers will vary. Possible responses include the following: Through singing (the collection of songs develops a church's sung theology of God and Christian faith); through rituals—rehearsing the communion ritual (words of institution); weddings (the ceremony rehearses the drama of the bride of Christ in union with Jesus Christ); observing seasons in the Christian year: advent, Christmas, Epiphany, Lent/Easter, Pentecost; telling the biblical stories and the ancient church associated with the seasons creates sacred memory of the Judeo/Christian faith.**

3. To what extent does your family or church use memory as a way to develop faith and Christian discipleship? **Answers will vary.**

4. If you were asked to describe the mission of your church, what story would you tell? **Answers will vary.**

"SO WHAT" - DIGGING DEEPER

1. In the eleventh century, before the invention of the printing press, churches were often constructed with large stained glass windows to tell biblical stories to people who could not read. What ways could churches tell biblical stories to non-readers today? **Answers will vary. Possible responses include the following: Banners and altar cloths—used to indicate seasons of the Christian year; specific colors signal the current season of the Christian year; Christian art; drama—plays, skits, and pantomime communicate well to non-readers; singing; liturgical dance or movement; videos—some churches use video announcements that shows how the church is fulfilling its Christian mission through service.**

2. Israel used feasts and festivals to conduct public remembrances of sacred events. Why do you believe it is important to gather in community to remember sacred events? **Answers will vary. Possible responses include the following: Corporate worship is an expected practice; remembering in community strengthens people's faith in ways that private devotions cannot; doing things in community**

reinforces the group's Christian identity as the body of Christ; remembering in community instills group ownership of the correct telling and retelling of the story.

3. The twelve stones were catalysts to prompt sacred storytelling. What prompts sacred storytelling in your home or congregation? **Answers will vary.**

CHAPTER 9

DISCUSSION

"WHAT" - THE BASICS

1. When facing a moral dilemma, what guides your thought process? Share any critical questions or moral framework that shape your thoughts. **Answers will vary.**

2. We often hear people diminish lying by saying something is a white lie. Would you say Rahab told a white lie? If not, how would you justify her actions? **Possible answers include the following: Common definitions of a white lie include a harmless lie, a lie with good intentions or a lie spoken to spare one's feelings. Rahab's response to the king of Jericho's men appears beyond these trivial characterizations of a lie. Rahab's choice to lie was a moral decision based on her faith (fearful reverence) for the God of Israel and for Israel through whom God defeated Pharaoh's Egypt, and the kings of Sihon and Og.**

3. Scripture says "The gates of Jericho were securely barred because of the Israelites. No one went out and no one came in." (Joshua 6:1) Why do you believe the king of Jericho wanted to bar Israel from entering Jericho's gates? **The king and the people of Jericho feared God and Israel and apparently were not willing to enter into alliance with them or God. Jericho was an established city with a protective wall. It clearly had the military advantage. The people may have believed they had the upper hand and did not need to welcome Israel or Israel's God.**

"SO WHAT" - DIGGING DEEPER

1. What from today's study of Rahab helped you understand the motives behind her decision to help the Israelite spies? **Answers will vary.**

2. Review God's instructions to Israel for the conquest of Jericho (Joshua 6:2-5). What do these unorthodox instructions teach you about God's strategy for overcoming Jericho? **Answers will vary. Possible responses include the following: God's unorthodox instructions require people to trust God's ways above human ingenuity and power. When one follows God's instructions, God gets the glory rather than people**

3. God instructed Israel to conduct a ritual ceremony (circling Jericho seven days, carrying the Ark of the Covenant, blowing trumpets by priests, and shouts from the larger community). What do you believe happened to the people

while they were participating in these moments? How has your participation in sacred rituals helped you or others through difficult situations? Share concrete examples. **Answers will vary. Possible responses include the following: The seven-day drama likely tested Israel's faith in God and provided opportunity for Israel's trust in God to build. It reinforced the nation's prioritization of God's guidance as its leader.**

CHAPTER 10

DISCUSSION

"WHAT" - THE BASICS

1. What about Joshua's covenant renewal speech do you believe most convinced Israel to renew their allegiance to God? **Answers will vary. Possible responses include the following: Joshua reminded Israel of her tendencies to follow foreign gods even though God delivered them from their enemies and led them to the Promised Land.**

2. Joshua's rehearsal of Israel's sacred history consisted of both positive memories (God's miraculous interventions) and negative memories (Israel's recurring worship of other gods). Which types of memories have most influenced you to examine your walk with God—the positive memories or the negative memories? Explain. **Answers will vary. Examine your reasons for answering the question as you did.**

3. Joshua challenged Israel to throw away the gods their ancestors worshiped. Why do you believe Joshua thought he could challenge Israel's spiritual integrity? **Answers will vary. Possible responses include the following: Joshua *knew* Israel. He had witnessed them indulge idols. They could not deny their shameful actions. Joshua's track record as a faithful leader gave him the credibility to demand spiritual integrity from Israel.** Whom would you allow to challenge your spiritual integrity? What are the implications of your response? **Answers will vary. Examine your reasons for answering the question as you did.**

"SO WHAT" - DIGGING DEEPER

1. Joshua urged Israel to revere the Lord, which means to walk with Him blamelessly, with integrity, and even with "perfection." Using concrete examples, explain what it means to revere the Lord. **Answers will vary. Possible responses include the following: Examining one's life in light of God's Word. Being consistent in word and deed. Being faithful to love God and others unconditionally.**

2. Joshua rehearsed Israel's history (the good and the bad parts) to help Israel take an honest look at how she had related to God over the years. What motivates you to take honest inventory of your walk with God? Share examples. **Answers will vary. Examine your reasons for answering the question as you did.**

3. Why do you believe Joshua was able to convince Israel to renew her covenant with God? Think about *what* Joshua shared with Israel and *how* he communicated his message. What did you learn from his method of persuasion? **Answers will vary. Possible responses include the following: Israel could not deny her participation in idol worship. The memory of God's deliverance reminded them of the favor they now enjoyed in a town they did not build. The reality that God could defeat them as God did Israel's enemies probably dawned on them. After weighing the options, Israel decided it was better to side with God.**

NOTES

NOTES